Inner and Outer Peace

Inner and Outer Peace

SRI CHINMOY

Peace Publishing • Montreal

ISBN 0-88497-769-2

CONTENTS

INTRODUCTION

*T*he peace of the world is the immediate concern of statesmen
and politicians. They struggle to contain conflict and prevent
the outbreak of a nuclear war, which would threaten the existence of the major cities of the world. Yet peace in its fullest dimen-
sions underlies the whole basis of life and is, therefore of wider
concern.

*In this book Sri Chinmoy, an Indian spiritual teacher, sheds light
on essential questions which involve the consideration of peace
from a spiritual viewpoint. He seeks to encourage the love of peace
in the hearts of men and to show that the creation from its divine
inception through to the human world is wrought in the peace and
in the love of its Creator. He shows that the seeds of destruction lie
in the individual psyche; that passions and the ego become tyrants
over the finer and nobler sensibilities when they are not checked by
the higher light of the soul. He affirms that the pursuit of peace at
its most fundamental level means being at peace with oneself.
When peace is conceived of only as the absence of conflict or as the
quiet rest of sleep, the aspiration for peace will not prove to be as
strong as the impulse to war.*

*Though mankind has the cumulative record of centuries of war
and conflict to remind itself of the nature of war, even this mighty
catalogue cannot check the perennial accretion of woe. Again and
again blood has inundated the earth. The refinements of civiliza-
tion have been reduced to dust in the pursuit of selfish ends and*

1

often in the aftermath, the debts of war have marred the enjoyment of peace.

Against this background, it would seem a little unrealistic to imagine that peace could consist merely in an absence of war; that would overlook the possibility that man might carry the seeds of future wars within himself. Similarly, it is hoping a good deal to imagine that peace can be preserved by nuclear disarmament, for, as long as the tendency to war prevails in the hearts of men, the weapons, once abandoned, can be reinvented and surpassed. The force of spirituality has the power to dissolve the reasons and, therefore, the weapons of war; it inspires a deep aspiration for peace.

Sri Chinmoy speaks of the higher truths which lift the peace of the world above purely political and historical considerations. When man looks upward to the teachings of religion and spirituality, he beholds life in a different light—it becomes more a spiritual yearning and pilgrimage than a battlefield between men. Sri Chinmoy gives new and contemporary expression to the truths about peace and life which can be found in the great classics of Indian spiritual philosophy. At a time when war threatens more destruction than ever before, he contributes his spiritual understanding and inspiration to the cause of world peace.

1

INNER
AND
OUTER
PEACE

INNER AND OUTER PEACE

*"There is no peace in the world today because
there is no peace in the minds of men."*
Secretary-General U-Thant

There is absolutely nothing as important as the search for peace in the outer world. Without peace the outer world is not only wicked to the backbone, but also hopelessly weak. Peace itself is strength. When you have inner peace, you can have joy and delight when you enter into the outer world. The outer world can be under your control when you have peace of mind, even if you have only a little peace of mind. Wherever you go, you will make your own peace. If you do not have any inner peace to offer, the only qualities you will express are restlessness and aggression.

The world is something very huge, but each person represents the world. You and I create the world by the vibrations that we offer to the world. Any little room, let us say, is a miniature world. If we can invoke peace and then offer it to somebody else, we will see how peace expands from one to two persons, and gradually to the world at large.

This world of ours has everything except one thing: peace. Everybody wants and needs peace, whether he be a child or an octogenarian. But the idea of peace is not the same for each individual. It sadly differs. The general in Eisenhower spoke on peace: "We are going to have peace, even if we have to fight for it."

The indomitable Napoleon voiced forth, "What a mess we are in now: peace has been declared." The Son of God taught us, "Blessed are the peacemakers, for they shall inherit the earth."

Somebody has very aptly said, "The more we strive for peace on earth, the more it seems that the dove of peace is a bird of paradise."

Each individual has his own way of defining peace. A child finds peace when he is running around outside. That is his fulfillment and in his fulfillment is his peace. An adult finds his peace somewhere else. He finds his peace when he feels that he can lord it over the world. And in the evening of life, an old man thinks that he will get peace if the world recognizes his greatness, or if Mother Earth offers her gratitude to him. He feels that he has done much for humanity and Mother Earth, and he expects something in return. He will have peace only if his expectation is fulfilled.

But peace can never dawn on any individual if it is not properly sought. The child cannot get true peace by running around in the street. He soon finds frustration in his so-called fulfillment. A day will come when he will pray to God for a calm and quiet life. Then he will have peace.

If an adult wants to have peace, real peace, he has to realise that he cannot get it by possessing the world or governing the world. It is only by offering what he has and what he is, consciously and unreservedly, to the world at large, that he will have peace.

The old man who will soon pass behind the curtain of eternity can have peace only if he cherishes the idea that he is not a beggar, but a king. He was a king and he still is a king. He has offered his inner and outer wealth to mankind and Mother Earth. If, in the evening of his life, he doesn't expect anything from the world, then his inner consciousness and outer being will be flooded with peace.

When you stand in front of the mirror, if you see an undivine face looking back at you, then rest assured that the whole world is undivine. But if you are getting joy from your face, if it is pure and divine, then rest assured that the world is also pure and divine. According to the way you see yourself, the rest of the world will present itself to you. If you see aspiration in your face, I assure you this aspiration you are bound to notice in the whole world. If you see aggressive forces, a devouring tiger inside you, then when you leave the house a big tiger will come and devour you. We are exact prototypes of the world. We are like a microcosm and the world is the macrocosm. A saint always sees everyone in the world—even the worst possible thief—as a saint. Similarly, a thief will see even the most divine saint as a thief. We judge others according to our own standard, according to our own realisation.

We want to please the world, but how can we please the world if we are not pleased with our own lives? It is sheer absurdity to try to please others if we are not pleased with our inner and outer existence. God has given us big mouths and we try to please others with our mouths, but inside our hearts there is a barren desert. If we have no aspiration, how can we offer the world peace, joy and love? How can we offer anything divine when we don't practise what we preach? Spirituality offers us the capacity to practise what we preach. If we don't follow the path of spirituality, we shall only preach; it will be a one-sided game. But if we really practise spirituality we shall also live the Truth. Our preaching will bear fruit only when it is practised.

Spirituality is the fount of world peace. Spirituality is the fulfillment of all responsibility. To love the world is our responsibility. To please the world is our responsibility. We know our own teeming responsibilities; but when we think of the world, unfortunately we do not think of it in a divine or proper way. The world immediately misunderstands us, and we find it impossible to have an inner connection with the world. It is like a mother and her son. In spite of her best intentions, the mother finds it difficult to please the son. She thinks of him in her own way and likewise, the son understands the mother in his own way. Because of this lack of communication the mother and the son get no joy in fulfilling their mutual responsibilities.

How can we fulfill all our responsibilities? We have tried in human ways but we have failed. We think of the world with good thoughts and ideas, but the world remains exactly the same as it was yesterday. We love the world, but the world still remains full of cruelty and hatred. We try to please the world, but the world doesn't want to be pleased. It is as if the world has taken a vow that it won't allow itself to be pleased. And why does all this happen? It is because we have not pleased our Inner Pilot, the One we have to please first. If we have no aspiration to please our Inner Pilot, how can we offer the world peace, joy and love? Unless and until we have pleased the Inner Pilot, the world will always remain a battlefield where the soldiers of fear, doubt, anxiety, worry, imperfection, limitation and bondage will fight; and consciously or unconsciously we will play with these undivine soldiers. Fear, doubt, anxiety, worry and animal propensities can never offer us peace, world peace.

Deep,deep within us divinity is crying to come to the fore. There the divine soldiers are our simplicity, sincerity, purity, humility and the feeling of oneness. These soldiers are more than ready and eager to fight with fear, doubt, anxiety and worry. Unfortunately, we are not consciously identifying ourselves with the divine soldiers; we are consciously or unconsciously identifying ourselves with the undivine soldiers, and that is why world peace is still a far cry.

We love the world. We have to love the world; it is our responsibility. What happens when we try to love the world or when we attempt to fulfill our responsibility to the world? We try to possess and bind the world, and while we are doing this we see that we have already been bound and are possessed by the world.

We have been seeing the desire for supremacy in man since the dawn of civilisation. Each human being wants to be an inch higher than the rest; each human being wants to surpass the rest.

But from the spiritual point of view, we can surpass only when we become one: one nation, one soul. One nation can surpass all the other nations only by becoming one with them in their suffering, in their joy and in their achievements. When we become one, we really surpass.

What do we surpass? We surpass not only the capacity of our own achievements and of others' achievements, but also the capacity of limited feelings.

From time immemorial, History has been dealing with tyrants and liberators. Before long, it will have to deal seriously with peacemakers. To be sure, peace is not the sole monopoly of heaven. Our earth is extremely fertile. Here on earth we can grow peace in measureless measure.

We can attain lasting inner peace only when we feel that our Supreme Pilot is in the many as one and in the one as many. When we consciously feel this truth in our life, we get lasting peace in whatever we say, whatever we do, whatever we offer and whatever we receive.

Once we have this inner peace, world peace can be achieved in

the twinkling of an eye. Inside, if we feel a good thought, an illumining and fulfilling thought, then that very thought we will
express and offer to our friends and dear ones. Our illumining,
soulful, fulfilling thoughts will enter into our dear ones and then
they, too, will have peace. So when we have inner peace,
automatically it expresses itself. It spreads its qualities or capacities
throughout the length and breadth of the world.

World peace will begin when the so-called human expectation
ends. World peace can dawn only when each individual realises the
Supreme Truth: Love is the revelation of life and life is the manifestation of love. World peace can be achieved, revealed, offered and
manifested on earth when in each person the power of love replaces
the love of power.

OUR PEACE IS WITHIN

"God is our refuge and strength, a very present help in trouble."

Old Testament

No price is too great to pay for inner peace. Peace is the harmonious control of life. It is vibrant with life-energy. It is a power that easily transcends all our worldly knowledge. Yet it is not separate from our earthly existence. If we open the right avenues within, this peace can be felt here and now.

Peace is eternal. It is never too late to have peace. Time is always ripe for that. We can make our life truly fruitful if we are not cut off from our source, which is the Peace of Eternity.

The greatest misfortune that can come to a human being is to lose his inner peace. No outer force can rob him of it. It is his own thoughts, his own actions, that rob him of it.

Our greatest protection is not in our material achievements and resources. All the treasure of the world means nothing to our soul's communion with the all-nourishing and all-fulfilling Peace. Our soul lives in peace and lives for peace. If we live a life of peace, we are ever enriched and never impoverished. Unhorizoned is our inner peace; like the boundless sky, it encompasses all.

Long have we struggled, much have we suffered, far have we travelled. But the face of peace is still denied us.

Peace is life. Peace is Bliss eternal. Worries — mental, vital and physical — do exist. But it is up to us whether we accept them or reject them. To be sure, they are not inevitable facts of life. Since our Almighty Father is All-Peace, our common heritage is peace. It is a Himalayan blunder to widen the broadway of future repentance by

10

misusing and neglecting the golden opportunities that are presented to us. We must resolve here and now that amidst all our daily activities we shall throw our heart and soul into the Sea of Peace. He is mistaken who thinks that peace will, on its own, enter into his life at the end of his life's journey. To hope to achieve peace without meditation and spiritual discipline is to expect water in the desert.

To have peace of mind, prayer is essential. Now, how to pray? With tears in our hearts. Where to pray? In a lonely place. When to pray? The moment our inner being wants us to pray. Why to pray? This is the question of questions. We have to pray if we want our desires or aspirations to be fulfilled by God. What can we expect from God beyond this? We can expect Him to make us understand everything, everything in nothing and nothing in everything: the Full in the Void and the Void in the Full.

We must always discriminate. We have to feel that the outer world which is attracting our attention is constantly fleeting. To have something everlasting, to attain a rocklike foundation in life, we have to turn toward God. There is no alternative. And there is no better moment to take that turn than when we feel most helpless.

To feel oneself helpless is good.
Better to cultivate the spirit of self-surrender.
Best to be the conscious instrument of God.

Everything depends on the mind, consciously or unconsciously, including the search for peace. The function of the mind is to remove the cloud of doubt. The function of purity in the mind is to destroy the teeming clouds of worldliness and the ties of ignorance. If there is no purity of the mind, there is no sustained success in the spiritual life.

We will own peace only after we have totally stopped finding fault with others. We have to claim the whole world as our very own. When we observe others' mistakes, we enter into their imperfections. This does not help us in the least. Strangely enough, the deeper we plunge, the clearer it becomes that the imperfections of others are our own imperfections, but in different bodies and minds. Whereas if we think of God, His Compassion and His

11

Divinity enlarge our inner vision of truth. We must come, in the fulness of our spiritual realisation, to accept humanity as one family.

We must not allow our past to torment and destroy the peace of our heart. Our good and divine actions can easily counteract our past bad and undivine actions. If sin has the power to make us weep, meditation has undoubtedly the power to give us joy, to endow us with Divine Wisdom.

Again, to pray to God for peace with full concentration and singleness of devotion even for five minutes is more important than to spend long hours in carefree and easy-going meditation.

Our peace is within. And this peace is the basis of our life. So from today let us resolve to fill our minds and hearts with tears of devotion, the foundation of peace. If our inner basis is solid, then no matter how high we raise the superstructure, danger can never threaten us. For peace is below, peace is above, peace is within, peace is without.

SPIRITUALITY

"...trailing clouds of glory do we come
From God, who is our home."
Wordsworth

Spirituality is at once a simple and a complicated word, a simple and, at the same time, complicated concept. Each individual has a special approach to spirituality.

Spirituality is truth-awareness. Spirituality is life-emancipation. Spirituality is oneness-manifestation. Spirituality is perfection-satisfaction.

There are two types of spirituality. One is false, totally false. The other is true, absolutely true. False spirituality tells us that we have to negate and reject life in order to reach Heaven or in order to achieve Peace, Light and Bliss in our human life. False spirituality tells us that we have to renounce everything if we really want Joy, Peace and Bliss in life and from life. True spirituality tells us that we must not reject anything, we must not negate anything, we must not renounce anything. True spirituality tells us that we have to accept everything. We have to accept the world as such and then we have to transform our inner world and our outer world for God-realisation, God-revelation and God-manifestation. It is only in God-realisation, God-revelation and God-manifestation that we can have boundless Peace, boundless Light, boundless Delight.

False spirituality is the dance of teeming desires. Desire is something that binds us to our possessions. There comes a time when we realise that although we are the possessor, we are actually slaves to our possessions. True spirituality is the song of aspiration. Aspiration liberates us from our binding and blinding possessions—

13

material possessions, earthly possessions, possessions that do not help elevate our consciousness to our life's true inner and outer goals.

False spirituality is desire. The acme of desire is this: "I came, I saw and I conquered. I came into the world, I saw the world and I have conquered the world. Now I am in a position to lord it over the world." The strangling vital, the demanding vital, the authoritarian vital wants this world for its enjoyment. But aspiration tells us something quite different. The teachings of aspiration are soulful, meaningful and fruitful. Aspiration tells us that each individual has come into the world to see, to love and to become inseparably one, to become fully aware of his universal existence. Mere individual existence is of no avail. One has to have a free access to the universal life within him.

Desire-life is the life of success; aspiration-life is the life of progress. The life of desire constantly demands, whereas the life of aspiration soulfully expects. The life of desire demands constantly from the world around us. The life of aspiration expects everything from the world within.

Success is short-lived satisfaction. Most of the time this short-lived satisfaction is followed by bitter dissatisfaction. In dissatisfaction what actually looms large is frustration; and frustration is the harbinger of total destruction. Progress is our continuous, illumining and increasing satisfaction within and without. Those who follow the spiritual life know and feel the supreme necessity of progress each day, each hour, each minute, each second. A seeker has to feel that he is making progress. He is running fast, very fast, towards his destined Goal. He is climbing high, speedily, towards his transcendental Goal. He is diving deep within extremely fast to reach the Absolute Lord in the inmost recesses of his heart.

In order to make progress each seeker has to have two satisfactory friends. These friends are always reliable, most reliable. Prayer and meditation are two most intimate friends of a seeker of the Absolute Truth. When the seeker prays to the Almighty Lord, he feels his Lord's presence high up in the skies above his head. He feels his Lord's existence above, far above, his mental vision—let us say in Heaven. In Heaven is his Lord Supreme. But when he meditates, he feels that his Lord Supreme is nowhere else except in his heart—in his loving, aspiring heart. His prayer tells him that his God is above. His meditation tells him that his God is within. When he reaches his Beloved on the highest plane of consciousness on the strength of his prayer, he enjoys the sweetest intimacy. He claims his Lord as his eternal Friend, his beginningless and endless friend. And when he reaches his Friend inside the very depth of his heart, he enjoys boundless ecstasy and delight in his Beloved Supreme.

Spirituality is the simplification of life. Spirituality is the glorification of life. When we are in the ordinary human life, there are countless problems. Every day we encounter these countless problems, and we find that there is no way to solve these problems or to simplify our complicated human life. But spirituality is our saviour. It comes to solve our problems, to simplify our complicated life; and again, it glorifies the divine in us. The divine in us is that very thing that wants to expand, illumine and fulfill the Immortal in us.

How do we simplify our life? Is there any specific way to simplify our complicated life? Yes, there is a way which enables us to simplify our most complicated life; and that is our concentration, our power of concentration. When we concentrate on our problems we come to notice that our power of concentration has actually come from a Source which is infinitely more powerful than all our problems put together. And this Source shows us how to simplify our problems. If we can concentrate on our problems even for five fleeting minutes, I wish to tell you from my own experience that this complicated world of ours will not remain complicated.

Once our complicated life is over, once our life of confusion and complication is over, we expect satisfaction from our lives. We naturally expect a life of peace and harmony. This world of ours has everything except one thing: peace of mind. If we have peace of mind, we do not need anything more from this world, from any individual or from ourselves. Now, how do we get peace of mind? The answer is the same: through spirituality, through meditation.

Spirituality has a most powerful hero-soldier. The name of that hero-soldier is meditation. If we know how to meditate for five minutes early in the morning before the day dawns, before the hustle and bustle of life begins, then we enter into a world of serenity, clarity, purity and finally peace—a world which is flooded with

15

peace. Each individual seeker has the potentiality, the capacity to meditate soulfully. Some may not know how to meditate immediately. It may take a few days or a few weeks or a few months. But no individual will forever remain unknowledgeable in the art of meditation. The art of meditation is something inherent in each individual.

So, meditation is the way to acquire peace of mind. Once we have established peace of mind, then in our day-to-day multifarious activities we shall enjoy boundless satisfaction. And in this satisfaction we shall notice progress—gradual, continuous, illumining and fulfilling progress. When we walk along the road of Eternity, what we need is progress. And inside our progress is God the ever-transcending Reality, which is the birthright of each individual seeker everywhere.

MEDITATION

"Silence is the element in which
great things fashion themselves."

Carlyle

We meditate for various reasons. Peace of mind we all badly need. Therefore, when we meditate, either consciously or unconsciously we aim at peace of mind. Meditation gives us peace of mind without a tranquilizer. And unlike a tranquilizer, the peace of mind that we get from meditation does not fade away. It lasts for good in some corner of the inmost recesses of our aspiring heart.

Meditation gives us purity. There are various ways to achieve purity. Some people advocate the traditional Indian system of breathing. By breathing systematically and also through some occult techniques of breathing in and out, one can definitely purify one's internal system to some extent. But this purity does not last permanently. However, when one prays and meditates soulfully and, at the same time, brings the soul to the fore, one is bound to achieve lasting purity. The purity that we get from our soulful meditation lasts forever in our aspiring consciousness.

When we pray, we feel either that we have done something wrong or that something can be invoked from above so that we do not do anything wrong. When we pray, we feel that the mistake-world is looming large. Either we have made a mistake by having done something or we have made a mistake by not having done something. Then our sincerity compels us to confess our mistake. So, prayer and confession very often go together.

But meditation does not believe in that kind of confession. Meditation says, "Why do you have to make a mistake and then

17

confess it? Do not remain near mistakes. Remain millions and billions and trillions of miles away from mistakes. Then you won't have to confess anything."

Meditation is not an escape exercise. When we pray, we try to bring down into us a higher reality or enter into a higher reality that will separate us from the world of suffering. We try to escape from the suffering of the world. But when we meditate, we do not try to escape. The seeker who meditates is a warrior, divine warrior. He faces suffering, ignorance and darkness, and inside the very life and breath of suffering he tries to establish the kingdom of Wisdom-Light.

The true seeker who meditates also knows that whatever he is doing is not for his own personal salvation. If everything that he is doing is only for his own salvation, then he and the world will always remain two different entities with two different ideals or goals. So, sincere seekers always try to assimilate world-truth, world-light and world-capacity and meditate for world transformation, illumination and perfection.

Real meditation never forces us to do something, to say something or to become something. It is the desiring vital or the desiring mind that enters into our meditation and forces us to try to achieve something. But meditation proper will never compel us to do something, to say something or to become something, for it knows that everything has to be natural and spontaneous. It only helps us enter cheerfully into the current of spiritual life.

Human life is beset with difficulties, dangers and so forth, but we can overcome these difficulties. We can take each difficulty as a powerful warning and we can take each warning as a blessing-light in disguise. The meditation-world invites us and leads us to the highest Reality. We see ahead a light, perfection-light. But as soon as we see this light that perfects us, we are frustrated. A red traffic light is frustration to us, especially when we are in a hurry to reach our destination. But we forget that it is the red light that saves our precious life from destruction. The red traffic light is regular and punctual. Regularly and punctually it is warning us, saving us. Similarly, regularity in meditation saves us, illumines us and fulfils us. The life of our outer smile is strengthened by the regularity of our prayer, and the light of our inner cry is increased by the regularity of our meditation.

When we meditate, we discover something and we invent something. From our regular meditation we discover faith inside us. This discovery we do not get from anything else. Immense, continuous, illumining and fulfilling faith we get only from our pure and sure meditation.

During our daily meditation we also invent. What do we invent? We invent gratitude. Our heart becomes the possessor of something which it did not possess previously, and that something is boundless gratitude. Each meditation creates a gratitude-flower inside our heart, and petal by petal this flower blossoms in worship of our beloved Lord Supreme. So we invent gratitude and discover faith from our meditation.

Meditation helps us hear the Voice of God. It not only helps us hear the Voice of God, but it also helps us listen to the Voice of God and the Choice of His Hour. After hearing the Voice of God, either we can stop or continue further and actually listen to the Voice. If we listen to the Voice of God, if we listen to the inner dictates at every moment, then the world of confusion that baffles us or that we ourselves create will no longer exist for us. The confusion-world we will no longer create for ourselves if we listen to the Voice of God.

There is a special way to listen to the Voice of God, and that special way is to meditate in silence. Silent meditation is the strongest force that can ever be seen, felt and executed. So silent meditation we must learn.

How do we meditate silently? Just by not talking, just by not using outer words, we are not doing silent meditation. Silent meditation is totally different. When we start meditating in silence, right from the beginning we feel the bottom of a sea within us and without. The life of activity, movement and restlessness is on the surface, but deep below, underneath our human life, there is poise and silence. So, either we shall imagine this sea of silence within us or we shall feel that we are nothing but a sea of poise itself.

Then, if we start meditating, we are bound to hear the Voice of God and we are bound to listen to the Voice of God. Once we become accustomed to listening to the Voice of God, at that time we feel that there is no tomorrow. There is no such thing as the future, there is no such thing even as today; it is all now. God is now; His Vision is now. The eternal Now is the only reality. In the eternal Now we grow and glow; in the eternal Now we please God, fulfil God and become perfect instruments of God.

2

THE STRUGGLE FOR PEACE

THE STRUGGLE FOR PEACE

"In His will is our peace."

Dante

It seems that right from the beginning of creation people have been saying that the world situation is very bad, very gloomy, and now some are using the term dangerous.

Forty years ago people heard the same message, and in ten years from now people will be saying the same things.

Before the dawn of civilisation and after the dawn of civilisation, what the world saw and has always seen has been an endless series of fights, battles and wars. Humanity could have easily avoided the destructive experiences of the past if it had longed for a higher vision and a deeper reality.

We are all aware of the undeniable fact that war results in victory and defeat. But this is a surface experience that covers our human mind and our human life. The inner experience is totally different. In the inner world, war is an immediate experience of separativity, and separativity is nothing short of tremendous loss in the world of oneness. Oneness alone can feed humanity's eternal hunger and bring about satisfaction. Those who cherish the body-reality's separation-consciousness are deplorable losers in the process of God's evolution in and through mankind.

Peace does not mean the absence of war. Outwardly two countries may not wage war, but if they inwardly treasure aggressive thoughts, hostile thoughts, that is as good as war. Peace means the presence of harmony, love, satisfaction and oneness. Peace means a flood of love in the world family. Peace means the unity of the

23

universal heart and the oneness of the universal soul.

In his outer being and inner being each man has only two realities: war and peace. Outer war we all know. We also know inner war. At every moment a sincere seeker has to fight against his own doubt, imperfections, limitations, bondage and death. This inner war is constant. The animal in man wars against peace in the outer world, in the world of conflicting ideas. The divine in man wars against ignorance in the inner world, in the world of mounting ideals.

Man invents war. Man discovers peace. He invents war from without. He discovers peace from within. War man throws. Peace man sows. The smile of war is the flood of human blood. The smile of peace is the love below, above.

Peace is the whole truth that wishes to enrapture humanity. War is the whole falsehood that wants to capture humanity. Peace begins in the soul and ends in the heart. War begins in the mind and ends in the body.

War forgets peace. Peace forgives war. War is the death of human life. Peace is the birth of the Life Divine. Our vital passions want war. Our psychic emotions desire peace.

Man seeks war when he thinks that the world is not his. Man invites war when he feels that he can conquer the world. Man proclaims war when he dreams that the world has already surrendered to him.

Man seeks peace because his earthly existence desperately needs it. Man welcomes peace because he feels that in peace alone is his life of achievement and fulfilment. Man spreads peace because he wants to transcend death.

We are crying for peace, but there are people who are dying for destruction. We may be crying for peace, but countless people live on earth and how many people are generally interested in peace? Very few. There are people on earth who want to destroy the world, who want to conquer other countries, to dominate. The world is vast, very vast. We are dying to bring about world peace, but it is like a homeopathic dose. Peace is not going to come in one day. The world will not be inundated with peace in a fleeting second. Similarly, the world will not be destroyed. Look at Hiroshima and Nagasaki, two small towns. The destruction was so powerful, but it didn't physically touch the rest of Asia.

The ancient dream of cooperation is not a human dream which has very little to do with reality. The ancient dream, to be precise, is not a dream at all but a faultless and divine vision—an unhorizoned vision—which is slowly, steadily and unerringly shaping the individual and collective destiny in humanity's march towards the supreme goal of universal oneness and transcendental newness. The world is evolving and progressing and reaching a higher standard of life. It is not moving in a horizontal way, but in a spiral. Therefore, at times this progress is not immediately noticeable. At times it confuses and baffles our human mind. But on the strength of our inner oneness with the world situation and world evolution, we see unmistakably the world's slow and steady progress.

True, man-made destructive forces are to be found here, there and everywhere. Here they may be in small measure; somewhere else, in large measure. But the creator of the wrong forces, the destructive forces, need not remain always a creator of wrong forces. He can easily become a creator of good forces. In spite of creating and possessing wrong forces, if one remains silent to catch a glimpse either consciously or unconsciously of the divine, illumining and fulfilling light, at that time one is taking the first step. The second step is to create positive realities in order to accelerate humanity's progress towards perfection.

A negative force is not by nature negative. Only it is a force that we use in a negative way. A knife can be used either as a destructive force or as a force of cooperation and oneness-expansion. With a knife one can stab others; with the same knife one can cut fruits and share them with others.

The ancient dream will always remain a new and progressive vision, for creation itself is an ever-transcending reality. We shall have to open our heart's door and our mind's windows in order to see from the body-room the light that illumines and fulfills the world around us. Then only we shall discover continual progress in humanity's march along Eternity's road to Infinity's Satisfaction-Goal.

The world situation, if it was bad, if it is bad now, and if it becomes worse has only one remedy and that is meditation, that is to say spirituality. If we pray and meditate, then we will be able to change the face and the fate of the world. This is the inner way.

There is no other way. With the inner way we get peace and the feeling of oneness. Once we can establish the feeling of oneness with the rest of the world there can be no war and no destruction.

THE ANSWER TO WORLD-DESPAIR

"Ah! when shall all men's good
Be each man's rule, and universal peace
Lie like a shaft of light across the land."
Tennyson

Before we offer the answer to world-despair, let us first try to know why there is world-despair. For if we do so, we shall be able to offer the most adequate answer to world-despair. Why is there world-despair? World-despair exists because the world desperately needs the life-illumining Light. Why is there world-despair? World-despair exists because the world constantly needs the life-energizing Love. Why is there world-despair? World-despair exists because the world immediately needs the life-immortalizing Delight.

The answer to world-despair is Light. The answer to world-despair is Love. The answer to world-despair is Delight. We need Light to see the Creator within and the creation without. We need Love to feel the Beloved within and the lover without. We need Delight to sail God's Boat within and to reach God's Shore without.

World-despair is at once bad and good, undivine and divine. It is bad and undivine because it lives in the darkness-palace of the ignorance-kingdom. It is good and divine because it cries for Light, more Light, abundant Light and infinite Light; Love, more Love, abundant Love and infinite Love; Delight, more Delight, abundant Delight and infinite Delight.

World-despair exists because there is a yawning gulf between our self-giving and the world's receptivity, between the world's self-giving and our receptivity. World-despair exists because there is a yawning gulf between our life-perfection and God's manifestation, between God's Life-Perfection and our manifestation.

Grace from above can be the only link between our self-giving and the world's receptivity and between the world's self-giving and our receptivity. Aspiration from below can be the only link between our life-perfection and God's manifestation and between God's Life-Perfection and our manifestation.

The absolute Grace of the Supreme has given birth to the transcendental Reality and the universal Reality. Man's constant inner cry reaches the transcendental Reality, which is the acme of Perfection in the world of the Beyond, and at the same time this inner cry manifests the universal Reality in the core of each aspiring individual on earth.

In the world of yesterday, ignorance guided and moulded us. In the world of today, despair lords it over us. In the world of tomorrow, glowing hope will guide us and lead us. And in the world of the day after tomorrow, we shall grow into God's Promise, the Promise of achievement immortal and infinite.

Talking, lecturing and advising the world can never be an adequate answer to world-despair. The most effective answer to world-despair lies in self-giving. But we learn the art of self-giving only after we have learned the art of self-finding. We learn the art of self-finding only after we have learned the art of meditating, the art of meditating on the Inner Pilot, the Supreme. What we call meditation is nothing other than God-manifestation. And God-manifestation, both within us and without us, is always a perfect stranger to human despair.

ON THE THREAT OF NUCLEAR DESTRUCTION

"Man drives, but God holds the reins."
Yiddish proverb

On the strength of my limited capacity, suppose I have painted, or let us say created a painting. I am the creator of that painting. Then you come, let us say, to destroy my painting. Will I not fight for my painting? Will I not feel, "Why do you have to destroy it?" Similarly, God the Creator created the creation, you and me. Here we are dealing with the Omnipotent, not with a human being, who is so limited. So God created this universe. It is His. Now you and I, thinking that we are very powerful, most powerful, will go and try to destroy His creation? Will He allow it?

I am an ordinary man. If I create something and you come, out of malicious pleasure, to destroy my creation I will fight for it, because I created it and you have no right to destroy it. Similarly, God the Creator has created us with His infinite Vision, His infinite Light and Delight. Now will He allow me or you, or anybody else, or all of us to destroy His creation? Will He allow us to destroy His creation, He being the Omnipotent? It is absurd.

When I create something, if you come to destroy it, I will fight for it. I will not allow you to destroy it, because it is my creation. So here, what right do we have to destroy God's creation? Again, let us say that we have become very undivine, we have become hostile forces and we want to destroy. But do we have the omnipotent power? God is the Omnipotent Power. He created us. Now His creation, you and I want to try to destroy. Look at God's Capacity and look at our capacity. Is it not ridiculous? At the right moment

He will simply change our mind.

Here is the switch for the atom bomb. Just switch it on and then the atom bomb will drop somewhere else, in some other part of the world. In our human mind, we can do it. Again, although I may have sent you to drop the bomb, if God wants to change your mind, in a fleeting second you will say, "O, no, I cannot do it. I do not want to do it. People are my brothers and sisters. I cannot do that! I cannot do that!" And then there is no atomic explosion.

I can brag for years and years that on the strength of my atomic research, atomic energy, I can destroy the world. But human capacity is so limited. The world is very vast, far beyond my imagination. Even if I want to destroy one little country, one little town or one little village, at that time, in a second if God enters into my mind, I will ask myself, "What am I doing?" The way God has entered into my heart and is making me feel that we are all one, brothers and sisters, making me feel that I cannot destroy, the same way, in a fleeting second, if God enters into my mind, my mind will act like the heart. I will not be able to destroy and I will not drop the atom bomb there.

SCIENCE AND SPIRITUALITY

*"In the heart of all things, of whatever there is
in the universe, dwells the Lord."*
The Upanishads

Man's scientific and spiritual achievements are the conscious inspiration-light and aspiration-might of the Divine's urge toward two goals: the realization of the body's countless necessities and infinite capacities, and the manifestation of the soul's transcendental vision of the Beyond here on earth, in the heart and immediacy of today.

Science is that precious thing on earth which is pushed forward by a glowing imagination and pulled forward by its own growing experience. Spirituality is that precious thing on earth which is carried within by fulfilling aspiration and later brought to the fore, where it can become consciously one with God the Field of Experience, God the Experience and God the Experiencer.

Within our living memory, we have seen science advancing very fast, while human happiness has been receding at an alarming rate. Today's world is seeing a flickering candle-flame of spirituality, but tomorrow's world will be flooded with the light of spirituality.

Science right now deals mostly with the material world. What is the material world, after all? It is the world that does not believe in the possibility and inevitability of a divine life. Spirituality right now deals mostly with the inner world. What is the inner world? The inner world is the world that says that the possibility of a divine life on earth is undoubtedly unreal today, but tomorrow it will be possible, the day after it will be practicable and just the day after that it will be inevitable.

31

Science has the capacity to show mankind the full development of the mental life. Spirituality has the capacity to show mankind the possibility and inevitability of the life beyond the mind, the supramental life.

The outer progress and world-discovery swiftly follow the fruitful imagination in the world of science. The inner progress and self-discovery gladly follow the soulful aspiration in the life of the world within, the world of spirituality.

Science and modern life are simply indispensable to each other. The modern life is the eye; science is the power of vision. Spirituality and the future life of mankind will be indispensable to each other. The future life of mankind will be the fully awakened consciousness, and spirituality will be its guiding and fulfilling soul.

Science itself has become an art, and this art must now stand alongside all other arts. No art can ever have its fullest expression in the modern world without the aid of science. Spirituality is the supreme art of our nature-transformation. God the Supreme Artist uses spirituality to divinely reveal to the world man's embodied divine Reality and transcendental Truth.

To fulfill his practical needs, man bitterly cries to science. To fulfill his personal inner needs, man helplessly cries to spirituality.

The somber despair of ruthless destruction and the matchless ecstasy of the outer, human fulfillment have a common friend: science. The most hopeful certainty of a new and pure creation and the life-energizing, life-nourishing, life-transforming and life-fulfilling delight of the inner and divine fulfillment have a common friend: spirituality.

Science and spirituality must be united. They need each other. Without the one, the other is incomplete, almost meaningless. Together they are not only supremely complete but also divinely meaningful. Science is the Body of God. Spirituality is the Soul of God. Science is also God the Body. Spirituality is also God the Soul. God the Body needs God the Soul to realize Himself, His Individuality. God the Soul needs God the Body to fulfill Himself, His Personality.

THE OUTER POWER AND THE INNER POWER

"One who knows others is wise; one who knows himself is wisest. One who conquers others is strong; one who conquers himself is strongest."
Tao Teh Ching

Each human being on earth embodies the outer power and the inner power. He is aware of his outer power when he looks without, around himself. He is conscious of his inner power when he dives deep within.

Each human being is the outer power and the inner power. When he calls himself the head and the body-consciousness, nothing more and nothing less, then he is the outer power. When he calls himself the soul, the soul-light, then he is the inner power.

The body-consciousness has light of its own. The soul-consciousness has light of its own. The body-consciousness, because of its limitations, does not see far. For the body-consciousness the future always remains a far cry. The soul-consciousness, because of its unlimited capacity, at one and the same time sees, grows into and becomes the achievements of the past, the realisations of the present and the vision-dreams of the future.

The outer power blinds the human in us. The outer power is devoured by the animal in us. The inner power clears and expands our vision; it shows our vision the way to reach the highest transcendental Goal.

The outer power is competition: conscious and constant competition. The inner power is conscious conception: conception of its own worth, its own reality and divinity. Divinity proceeds and succeeds, succeeds and proceeds. Reality eternally is. Again, in its silence-life, reality is at once the transcendental Height and the immanence-Light.

The outer power is supremacy. The inner power is accuracy: accuracy stating the fact of what it has and what it is. What it has is the source and what it is, is the manifestation of the source.

The outer power sings with imagination, dances with temptation, dies in frustration. The inner power is concentration, meditation and contemplation. Concentration accepts the challenges of life. Meditation purifies and illumines the challenges of life. Contemplation transforms the challenges of life into golden opportunities in life for the inner being, the Inner Pilot in us.

The outer power wants to strike and then immediately wants to escape. The inner power wants not only to embrace the world but also to convince the world that the world's existence and its own existence are eternally inseparable.

The outer power says to the inner power, "Look what I have. I have the capacity to destroy God's entire creation." The inner power says to the outer power, "Look what I have. I have the power to illumine God's entire creation."

The outer power is at times afraid of its own creation: the atom bomb and the hydrogen bomb. The inner power is constantly feeding its creation with love-light, concern-light and perfection-light.

The outer power feels that there is a height which has to be transcended and that if this goal is achieved, then satisfaction will dawn. The inner power feels that height and depth, the foot of the mountain and the top of the mountain, are all at one place. It sees that they are singing the song of one reality, that they are all inside the cosmic Heart in perfect union, enjoying inseparable oneness.

The outer power wants only to ascend. It is afraid of descending. The inner power wants to ascend and descend. It knows perfectly well that when it is descending, it is carrying down to earth the descending God; and when it is ascending, it is carrying up to Heaven the ascending God.

The outer power is the dance of sound. The inner power is the song of silence. The life of sound is the creation of the human in us. The life of silence is the creation of the divine in us. The human in us wants to prove its existence. It feels that unless and until it can prove its existence, the world will have no respect for us, the world will not care for us. The divine in us does not want to prove its existence for world-acceptance, world-appreciation and world-admiration. The divine in us feels that its existence is God's universal existence. God is experiencing His own ascending, descending and transcending Light in the divine in us.

The outer power is the human power. The inner power is the divine power. The outer power says, "I can do. I need no help, no assistance." The inner power says, "I can do nothing and I am nothing. At the same time, I can do everything because there is someone in me, the Inner Pilot, who will do everything for me." Furthermore, it says that the Inner Pilot has already done everything for us and that we only have to be aware of this.

When we live in the desire-world, the outer power lords it over us. The desire-world is the world of possession and frustration. When we live in the aspiration-world, the inner power illumines us and fulfills us.

The desire-world is the world without. The aspiration-world is the world within. Realisation has a free access to the inner world. And what is realisation? Realisation is the acceptance of reality as it is, reality at its present stage of evolution and reality at its ultimate height. Realisation tells us that the animal in us is for transformation, the human in us is for perfection, the divine in us is for manifestation.

3

THE PATH TO PEACE

THE PATH TO PERSONAL PEACE, PART 1

"Peace is indivisible"
                                          Litvinov

What is peace? Peace is our liberation from bondage. What is liberation? Liberation is our universal oneness with God the Unity and God the Multiplicity. What is bondage? Bondage is the dance of our unlit ego. What is ego? Ego is the unreal in us. And what is the real in us? The real in us is Truth; the real in us is God. God and Truth are inseparable, the obverse and reverse of the same coin.

What is peace? Peace is our satisfaction. What is satisfaction? Satisfaction is our conscious and constant oneness with the Will of the Supreme Pilot. Where does this satisfaction lie? It lies in our self-giving and in our God-becoming.

Peace, the world needs. We all need peace. But when we think of peace we try to discover it in our mind. We feel that peace can be found only in the mind, and if once we can discover peace in the mind, then our problems will be solved for good. But at this point I wish to say that the mind we are referring to is the physical mind. The mind is the doubting mind, and in the doubting mind we can never feel the presence of peace. We can feel the presence of peace only in the loving heart. The doubting mind leads us to total frustration. The loving heart leads us to complete satisfaction. We doubt, and then we feel a barren desert within us. We love, and then we feel a sea of Reality and Divinity within us.

Peace is not to be found in external knowledge. Most of our external knowledge is founded on information, and information cannot give us any abiding satisfaction. Peace is not to be found in

39

outer efficiency. Peace is found in self-mastery.

If we want to achieve peace in our inner and outer life, then we must know the necessity of reciprocal inclusiveness and not mutual exclusiveness. Earth and Heaven must be united. Heaven has the silence of the soul. Earth has the sound of life. The silence of the soul leads us to our Source, the highest Reality; and the sound of life allows us to manifest what is within that highest Reality. In the inclusiveness of earth and Heaven we can achieve peace.

Peace is the only authority in our life of ascent and descent. When we ascend, we learn the song of unity in multiplicity. When we descend, we learn the song of multiplicity in unity.

Peace is our inner wealth. The inner wealth we can bring to the fore only when we expect nothing from the outer world and every-thing from the Supreme Pilot within us, at God's Choice Hour. Often, when we work for the world and serve the world we feel that it is the world's bounden duty to offer us gratitude or to acknow-ledge our service. When we expect something from the world, we are bound to meet with frustration. But when we expect from the Inner Pilot, He fulfils us beyond the flight of our imagination. But one thing we must know, and that is that God has an Hour of His own.

Our duty is to pray for peace, meditate on peace, concentrate on peace and contemplate on peace. God's duty is to inundate us with His Peace. When we know the art of surrender, the kingdom of peace within us cannot separate itself from our living reality. It is our conscious inner surrender, our unconditional surrender to the Inner Pilot that expedites our journey toward the discovery of the all-illumining and all-fulfilling Peace.

THE PATH TO PERSONAL PEACE, PART 2

*"God for His service needeth not proud work of
human skill; They please Him best who labour
most in peace to do His will."*
Wordsworth

Without peace we do not and cannot live like true human beings.
We desperately need peace—peace within, peace without. So how is
it that we do not have peace, which is so important in our life? We
do not have peace because of our hunger for possession. We want
to possess the world. But is there anything on earth which we can
claim as our own, very own? We can consider something to be our
possession only when we have the last word about it, only if
whatever we say goes. But even the members of our own reality-
existence—our body, vital and mind—don't listen to us and are not
within our control. Instead, they try to control us.

We want our body to be active, but our body wants to wallow in
the pleasures of lethargy. We want our vital to be dynamic, but
instead our vital becomes aggressive and tries to destroy others. We
want our mind to be inundated with faith, but instead our mind
always doubts and suspects. It is inundated with doubt at every moment. It not only doubts others, but it also doubts its own capacities, its own achievements, its own realities, its own realisations.
This moment the mind will say that you are a very good person.
The next moment the same mind will say that you are very bad. The
following moment the mind will wonder, "Am I right in doubting
that person?" First we say that someone is nice; next we say that
that same person is bad. Then we start doubting our mind's
capacities. Once we start doubting the reality and the authenticity
of our mind, destruction starts. When we doubt someone else, we

41

may not gain or lose anything very significant. But when we start doubting ourselves, then our reality-life comes to an end. If we do not have peace of mind, then how will we have happiness? If one part of the being remains without peace—either the heart, the mind, the vital, or the physical—then happiness will remain a far cry. Real peace—divine peace, illumining peace, fulfilling peace—is bound to give us happiness when the entire being is inundated with it.

If we can't control our own body, our own vital or our own mind, then how do we dare to claim these as our own? Even if we say that they are our possessions, we see that death will eventually come to snatch them away. The things that we cannot keep permanently, we cannot claim as our own possessions. So how can we renounce them? The very idea of renunciation is ridiculous because we do not have anything to renounce. If we dive deep within, we see that we are veritable beggars. How can a beggar renounce anything?

So possession brings frustration, and renunciation is fruitless. What, then, can give us peace? Only acceptance of God's Will can give us true peace. In our heart, in our life, there is only one ultimate prayer, the prayer that the Saviour Christ has taught us: "Let Thy Will be done." Millions of prayers have been written from time immemorial, but no prayer can equal this one: "Let Thy Will be done." When we accept God's Will as our own, at every moment peace looms large in our life of wisdom, in our life of aspiration and in our life of dedication.

How can we know something is God's Will? When something is God's Will, we will feel a kind of inner joy or satisfaction even before we start doing it. While working, we will also get joy. Finally, we feel that we will be equally happy if our action is fruitful or fruitless. In the ordinary life we are happy only when success dawns. Only when we see victory at the end of our journey are we happy and delighted. But if we can have the same kind of happiness, joy and satisfaction whether we succeed or fail, and if we can cheerfully offer the result of our actions at the Feet of our Beloved Supreme, then only can we know that what we have done is God's Will. Otherwise, when there is success, we feel that what we did was God's Will, and when there is failure, we say that what we did was the will of a hostile force. Or when we succeed we say it is because of our personal effort, our will, and when we fail we say it is because God does not care for us.

To have peace in abundant measure, we have to surrender our earth-bound will to the Heaven-free Will of God. We have to cheerfully, soulfully, devotedly, unreservedly and unconditionally surrender our limited human reality to the universal or transcendental Reality. This surrender is not like the surrender of a slave to his master. This surrender is based on the wisdom-light that recognises a difference between our own highest height and our own lowest depth. Both the highest and the lowest belong to us. When we surrender our will to the Will of the Supreme, we offer our lowest part to our highest part, for the Supreme is none other than our own highest Self.

We are like a tiny drop, and God, our Source, is like the vast ocean. When the drop enters into the ocean, it loses its limited individuality and personality and becomes the ocean itself. Again, it does not actually lose anything; it only increases its existence-light unimaginably. Similarly, if we maintain our own individuality and personality, we will always be assailed by fear, doubt and other negative and destructive qualities. But when we enter into the Source, which is all light and delight, at that time we acquire all the divine qualities and capacities of the Source. In this way, when we surrender our lowest self, which we now represent or embody, to our highest Self, we get peace and our entire being is inundated with joy, light and delight.

Right now fear, doubt, anxiety, tension and disharmony are reigning supreme. But there shall come a time when this world of ours will be flooded with peace. Who is going to bring about the radical change? It will be you: you and your sisters and brothers, who are an extension of your reality existence. It will be you and your oneness heart, which is spread throughout the length and breadth of the world.

THE PATH TO WORLD PEACE

*"I can think of no worthier task than that of
creating the tools for international co-operation
and working for the betterment of his fellow
human beings."*
Secretary-General U-Thant

Each nation has a soul of its own. The soul is at once God's illumining activity and the nation's fulfilling capacity. Each nation is the involution of its highest Light and the evolution of its inmost Power. Immortality is the homeland of the soul. Eternity is the life of the soul. Infinity is the reality of the soul.

When a nation's outer life listens to the inner dictates of its soul, its earthly desires decrease, its heavenly aspirations increase, its human wants are lessened and its divine needs are heightened. It envisions the Truth transcendental and grows into God's Pride supreme.

The great philosopher Arthur Schopenhauer once remarked, "Every nation ridicules other nations, and all are right." It is true that all nations, with no exception, will one day be flooded with God's perfect Perfection, at God's choice Hour. The nations that are aspiring consciously are hastening God's Hour. The nations that are aspiring unconsciously are inwardly valuing God's Hour, and soon their aspiration will increase. The nations that are wallowing in the pleasures of darkening and darkened night are God's so-called failures, but before long even they will open their eyes and, along with their forerunners will hear God ringing the bell of Inner Victory.

The ascending aspiration of the fully awakened souls and the descending Blessing-Light of God can eventually transform the face of the entire globe.

Imperfection and impossibility we cherished yesterday. Today, imperfection and impossibility are our unwanted guests. Tomorrow, they will be seen nowhere. Perfection and divinity will be our most welcome guests.

The nation that soulfully cries for inner development and devotedly cries for outer growth can alone be in the vanguard of the teeming nations. Why does a nation fail? A nation fails because it does not want the sustaining Truth to be on its side. When does a nation fall? A nation falls when it deliberately and vehemently resists the idea of being on the side of Truth. How can a nation succeed? A nation can succeed by following the Truth within and without. The very pursuit of Truth can make the existence of a nation free, meaningful, purposeful and fruitful. Now, how can a nation flourish? A nation can flourish when it sees no difference between the Creator and the creation. A nation can flourish when it loves the world, not for what the world will give in return, but for the sake of love. Selfless love, true love, never ends, never fails. Love is its own immediate reward.

To me, the real worth of nations lies in their united principles; and it is in the united principles that one can see the fruit of true inner oneness and divine perfection. The united principles must have co-operation. If there is no co-operation, then the united principles will bear no fruit whatsoever. The present-day world needs co-operation.

At the United Nations we can see the promising hearts of one hundred and twenty-five nations. Each nation is unique, for in and through each nation the Lord Supreme wants to fulfill Himself. Each nation is chosen by the Supreme, to fulfill Him in an unprecedented, unique manner.

We have to know whether we shall always remain with mere promise or whether we shall go one step ahead. That step is commitment. There is a great difference between promise and commitment. Promise can be a mere word, a meaningless, fruitless and lifeless gift. But inside commitment the illumining reality and fulfilling reality abide.

The promises that we have made to God and to mankind must be transformed into conscious, constant and unconditional commitments. It is inside the heart of commitment that all the promises of the past, present and future can blossom into fulfilling reality.

Each nation right now needs peace. We all need peace. To have peace, what we need is the right path, the Path Divine.

The inner heart of the United Nations is flooded with peace. The outer heart of the United Nations is trying to spread peace all over the world.

The outer existence of the United Nations is a colossal hope. The inner existence of the United Nations is a fulfilling reality.

The heart of the United Nations has peace. The body of the United Nations is for peace. The mind of the United Nations seeks peace. The vital of the United Nations needs peace.

The presence of peace in the heart is divine oneness. The presence of peace in the mind is divine illumination. The presence of peace in the vital is divine dynamism. The presence of peace in the body is divine satisfaction. Peace we need. Man seeks peace because he needs peace desperately. Man welcomes peace because it is in peace alone that he can have his own true achievement and fulfillment. Man needs peace. He has to spread it. The moment he needs peace, he has to feel that sooner or later he will receive it. He has to feel that his inner being will be flooded with peace. But he has to spread this peace. Man spreads peace because he knows that he has to conquer and transcend death.

The goal of the United Nations is peace, world peace. The secret of the United Nations is sacrifice.

There are two types of people: one wants peace, the other does not. Many nations have formed the outer body of the United Nations. Peace is expected from each nation in abundant measure. The Supreme loves all nations, because all are marching towards the same Goal. But if any nation wants to outdo other nations ruthlessly, then that particular nation will never be claimed by God's pride, heaven's delight and earth's gratitude as their own. When all nations work together devotedly and untiringly, then only can they embody universal oneness and reveal universal love.

The power that dominates cannot solve world problems. The power that loves can solve world problems. It is this power that binds its fulfilment and self-giving. Self-giving is done not with a sense of sacrifice but with the feeling of the whole as one real reality. The power that feels insufficient, inadequate in the absence of one member of the world community can solve world problems. The power that declares "united in the heart's world we stand: divided in the mind's world we fall," can easily solve world problems.

THE UNITED NATIONS AND WORLD UNION

"Blessed are the peace-makers."
New Testament

The United Nations is the seed. World union is the fruit. Both are equally important; both are of supreme importance. God-Vision embodies the seed. God-Reality reveals the fruit.

The United Nations is the morning. World union is the day. When the heart of the morning is flooded with inner light, divine light, the Light of God, then it is not only possible but almost certain that the entire day will be flooded with light. On very, very rare occasions we see otherwise. But most of the time morning shows the day.

The United Nations tells us where truth is. World union tells us what truth is. Where is truth? Truth is in self-giving. What is truth? Truth is man's transformation of his earth-bound nature.

The United Nations is a group of pilgrims on a journey. As the pilgrims walk along the path of light toward the same destination, they feel mutual appreciation. From appreciation they go one step ahead to love. From appreciation comes love and from love comes oneness. Oneness is the perfection of man in God and the satisfaction of God in man. He who is a true member of the United Nations treasures a shared life in a shared world.

A divided mind and a separated heart cannot quench the inner thirst either of the United Nations or of the world. We must cultivate a new type of reality, a new type of truth. This truth is creative, illumining and fulfilling. This truth must awaken the dormant physical in us, marshal the unruly vital in us, illumine the doubtful and suspicious mind in us and strengthen and immortalise the insecure heart in us. This truth is world union.

Each individual must dive deep within and discover his pent-up reservoir of dynamic energy. This energy has to be released so that the human mind can enter into the universal Mind, so that the human heart can enter into the eternal Heart and so that the human life can enter into the Life immortal.

Both the United Nations and the world have a special type of faith. This faith is evolutionary. It evolves from within to without, it evolves from unity to multiplicity and it evolves from multiplicity into the transcendental Reality.

The United Nations and world union have an evolutionary faith and a revolutionary life. This revolutionary life wants to challenge the untold poverty and teeming ignorance of the world. The golden day is bound to dawn when this world of ours will be totally freed from poverty. But the outer poverty can be transformed only when the inner poverty is removed. Inner poverty is our lack of faith in our divine reality, our lack of faith in our capacity to realise the ultimate Truth. Unless and until we have put an end to our inner poverty, the problem of the outer poverty cannot be solved.

Inner poverty is disharmony and restlessness; inner plenitude is peace, harmony and love. For the lover of the United Nations and world union, the watchword must needs always be peace. Peace is found in self-giving and in our recognition of others' good and divine qualities. The more we see the divine qualities in others, the sooner we will establish world peace.

Each nation has the strength and willpower of the Absolute. Each nation has the golden opportunity in the inner world to offer to the outer world a living hope and a living promise. This hope and this promise are not a mental hallucination or a false aggrandisement of ego. They are an inner reality that the nation can easily bring to the fore. In the inner world all the nations are equally important, for in the inner world each nation has a free access to world peace, world light, world harmony and world perfection. But in the outer life the nations that consciously aspire and cry for light are in a position to help the less advanced nations that are walking behind.

In the evolutionary process of human life, the first rung of the ladder is the United Nations, the second rung is world union and the third rung is man's total and perfect Perfection. But if we do not place our foot on the first rung and then on the second, it will be simply impossible for us to climb up to the Highest.

Each nation is a promise of God for God Himself. What we call world union today has to be surpassed tomorrow by something else, and that something else is world perfection. Union as such is not enough; the perfection of union is what we actually want. We may stay in a family even if we quarrel, fight and kill one another. But only if we can establish the sweetest feeling of oneness, does our union reach the acme of perfection.

EAST AND WEST

"The truly wise live peacefully and impartially.
In their eyes people share a common heritage.
The truly wise accept all people
as their own family"
Tao Teh Ching

The East is spiritual, the West is material. The East cries for the transcendental Spirit, the West cries for the universal matter.

The East is in the heart and for the heart. The West is in the mind and for the mind. The East from within comes to the fore and flowers. The West from the outer existence goes deep within and flowers.

The East wants silence. The West wants sound. Silence embodies the teeming Vast eventually to proceed. Sound inspires the teeming Vast continuously to succeed.

This world of ours is beset with countless problems. The spiritual East thinks that the Beyond is the only answer. The material West thinks that the answer is to be found here on earth; it thinks that the answer is: live and enjoy and enjoy and live.

The East believes in fate because it believes in reincarnation. The West does not believe in reincarnation; therefore, it does not believe in fate.

We can endlessly see and determine the differences between the East and the West. But the real question is whether these differences are being synthesized or not. At the very beginning, if we know what the heart can offer and what the mind can offer, then it will be an easy task to synthesize the two. The heart wants to see the oneness, feel the oneness and become the oneness itself. The mind wants diversity in the vital and multiplicity in the mind proper. The heart knows that there is a road that leads upward. The mind knows

51

that there is a road that leads forward. The East wants to walk along the road that leads upward. The West wants to walk along the road that leads forward.

The synthesis between East and West starts because of their feelings of insufficiency. The East sees that if it does not accept the material life, then it will not be able to manifest what it inwardly has. The West feels that if it does not accept the spiritual life, then it will not have a solid foundation. Then everything can be easily shattered.

The East has already gained considerable knowledge and wisdom from the West, especially in the scientific world. The West has gained considerable knowledge and wisdom from the East, especially in the spiritual world. Here we see that the heart and the mind cannot function separately and individually. They have to function together, provided they feel the need of an integral perfection in life. The mind without the heart will not know what the supreme Reality is. The heart without the mind will not know how the supreme Reality can be manifested here on earth. To our great joy, the East and the West are constantly complementing each other to make each other perfect consciously, and more so unconsciously.

The East is like the body of a bird and the West is like the wings of a bird. If the bird does not spread its wings, then how will it fly? And again, when it flies and reaches the highest Height, at that time it has to know that there is another goal and that goal is God-Manifestation on earth. There are two goals: one goal is Heaven-reality and the other goal is earth-reality. When we use the wings to go upward to the heavenly goal, we go with the earth-reality to the Heaven-reality. And when we come down to the earthly goal, we come down with the Heaven-reality to the earth-reality. It is like climbing up and down a tree. We climb up a mango tree and pluck mangoes, and then bring them down and distribute them. The East says, "Gather!" The West says, "Spread!" If we do not gather, then how can we spread? Only if we gather can we spread. Again, if we spread what we have, then the Source is pleased with us and the Source gives us everything in infinite measure.

Perfection only can give humanity abiding satisfaction. So the East, instead of rejecting, gladly accepts the great possibilities, capacities and realities of the West. The West too does exactly the same. They are combining their possibilities and transforming these possibilities into divine practicabilities with the hope that supreme satisfaction will dawn in the all-embracing and all-illumining common realisation of East and West.

We will have a harmonious, happy world-society only if this synthesis continues, and we can take East and West as the two arms, two eyes, two feet and two legs of the Supreme Pilot within and without. The other human divisions and distinctions—racial, cultural and linguistic—are destined to disappear from the human consciousness when it is flooded with a higher Light. This is the inevitable consequence of the Hour of God that is dawning all over the world. When the Hour of God appears, diversities will be there, but these diversities will be enriched and enhanced in fullest measure. And they will not disturb the general consciousness; on the contrary, they will harmoniously complement the whole. Humanity will be a true human family in every sense of the term and also in a sense that the human mind has yet to discover. And here I wish to say that this discovery will exceed all human expectations.

The awakened consciousness of man is evolving towards the Divine Existence. This is a most hopeful streak of light amidst the obscurities of the present-day world. This is a moment when human beings do not only join hands, but also join minds, hearts and souls. All physical, vital and mental barriers between East and West will dissolve, and high above national standards, above even individual standards, we shall see the supreme banner of divine Oneness.

FREEDOM

"My angel — his name is Freedom —
Choose him to be your King;
He shall cut pathways east and west,
And fend you with his wing."

Emerson

There is nobody who does not need freedom. At the same time, there is not a single person who has freedom in abundant measure. We need freedom from ignorance, bondage and death. Now, our freedom is our conscious, constant and unconditional acceptance of the Will of our Inner Pilot. Our freedom is God's Heart of Compassion. Our freedom is the manifestation of His Will here on earth. Our freedom lies in our service and in our dedicated life.

We love; therefore we are free. How do we love? We love through our self-offering. Why do we love? We love because God, our Source, is all Love.

We serve; therefore we are free. How do we serve? We serve devotedly and unreservedly. Why do we serve? We serve precisely because we wish to expand our heart and heighten our life.

We are detached; therefore we are free. We are detached because of our awareness of the fact that we are not indispensable in anybody's life. We tried being attached to others, but we found that this attachment in no way relieved them from their sufferings; on the contrary, it only added to their ignorance-night.

But we do feel that there is someone who is indispensable, and that someone is the Inner Pilot. Our devotion to the supreme Inner Pilot is the thing of paramount importance in our life. On the physical plane some may see this as attachment, but on the spiritual plane all will know that it is devotion to the supreme Cause. When we pay all attention to the Light within and above, we call it devotion. Since we are devoted to the Supreme, it is our bounden duty to inspire others to devote themselves to the same Inner Pilot if so He wills.

Here we are all seekers; we are all seekers of freedom-light. Once we become freedom-seekers, we know freedom represents our conscious satisfaction in a life of constant frustration. Although we are wedded to ignorance-night and constantly suffer from excruciating inner pangs, still we feel there is a streak of light in our life, and this light is our ever-growing, ever-expanding inner freedom.

Ignorance-night tells us that we are building castles in the air, that there is no abiding truth in our conception of Light, no reality in our feelings. Ignorance says that we are of night and we should be all the time for night. But our inner freedom tells us that today we are of God and for God, and that tomorrow God will make us future Gods. It tells us that God wants us to be equal to Him in every possible way. He feels that if we are an inch below Him, then He cannot manifest His Divinity, Eternity and Immortality to the fullest extent. Only when we are on the same footing as God can His divine Enjoyment reach the acme of perfection.

Freedom is peace. Peace is an inner experience of our totality. Totality is the silence-sound and the sound-silence of Reality. When the sound-silence ascends, we realise our true Self. When the silence-sound descends, it is time for God-manifestation. We ascend with sound-silence, and that is our God-realisation. We descend with silence-sound, and that is our God-manifestation.

Freedom is simplicity. Simplicity does not mean the absence of complexity; it in no way stands against complexity. Simplicity is our conscious acceptance of our own integrality. Freedom includes and it excludes. It excludes hunger from our human existance. It includes the divine feast that we constantly enjoy with the Lord Supreme in our divine existence.

Freedom is purity. Purity expedites our divine journey toward the transcendental Goal. It constantly, consciously and devotedly makes us feel what we are and what we are not. What we are is God's chosen children, seeking to manifest Him unconditionally in His own Way here on earth. What we are not is the chosen children of ignorance.

Freedom constantly reminds us that our Source is Light, and

that our existence can therefore be nothing but a flood of Light. We realise the authenticity of this statement only when we dive deep within and feel the necessity of listening to the dictates of our inner being. Freedom reminds us of the supreme fact that our divine Source is eternal and our existence here on earth is going to be supremely divine. It is a matter of time. At God's choice Hour, today's imperfection is bound to blossom into tomorrow's perfect Perfection.

The human in us feels that freedom is the fulfilment of our individuality. But when the human in us aspires, it comes to realise that this kind of freedom is nothing but earthbound individuality. The divine in us sees and feels that real freedom is the experience of universal reality or universality itself. As the ordinary person feels that his freedom is his individuality, the aspiring person feels that his freedom is his universality. And the Supreme in us feels that the real freedom lies in our all-embracing, all-illumining and all-fulfilling love for the world which is within us, which is without us, which is all-where.

We are all human beings. Most of the time we dwell in the world of hope. Hope is right now by far our best friend. When we hope for freedom, we know that it is our human friend, our human realisation, that is speaking within us. Hope for freedom is our human realisation. Promise for freedom is our divine realisation. Finally, our will for freedom, our adamantine will power, is our supreme realisation. Freedom we need, precisely because the Inner Pilot within us wants us to be free, totally free from the meshes of ignorance. Only then can we sing, dance and play with Him in His garden of ever-blossoming, ever-illumining and ever-fulfilling Dream and Reality.

4

THE MESSAGE OF THE UNITED NATIONS

THE MESSAGE OF THE UNITED NATIONS

"No more war; war never again! Peace.
His peace which must guide the destinies of
people and of all mankind."

Pope Paul VI

The outer message of the United Nations is Peace. The inner message of the United Nations is Love. The inmost message of the United Nations is Oneness. Peace we feel. Love we become. Oneness we manifest.

The United Nations has a mind, a heart and a soul. Its mind tries to offer flowing Peace. Its heart tries to offer glowing Love. Its soul tries to offer fulfilling Oneness. In the near future, a day will dawn when the message of the United Nations will be absorbing to the child, elevating to the common man, thought-provoking to the highly educated and inspiring to the seeker.

Each delegate is a force. Each representative is a force. Each nation is a force. The source of this force is a particular will. This will can be either the Divine Will or the human will. The human will wants to be with the world and in the world only on one condition: that it will be able to gain supremacy over others and maintain this supremacy. The Divine Will wants to be in the world, with the world and for the world without expecting anything from the world. The human will, at most, tolerates the world. The Divine Will constantly wants to liberate and fulfil the world. The human will wants to control and lead the world. The Divine Will wants to transform, glorify and immortalise the world. The human will in us needs the soul's expanding and illumining purity. The Divine Will in us wants the Goal's blossoming divinity.

The League of Nations was a dream-seed. The United Nations is a reality-plant. The aspiring and serving life of man's universal oneness will be the eternity-tree.

The goal of the United Nations lies not only in thinking together, but in thinking alike. Each individual has every right to love his nation; but he must also dedicate himself in order to immortalise his nation's relationships, inner and outer, with the rest of mankind, so that all can run together for the universal good of humanity.

In the words of Pope John XXIII:

"It is our earnest wish that the United Nations organization may become ever more equal to the magnitude and nobility of its tasks, and that the day may come when every human being will find therein an effective safeguard for the rights which derive directly from his dignity as a person, and which are therefore universal, inviolable and inalienable rights."

All nations together can build a temple. All nations together can make a shrine. All nations together can worship a Deity. At the entrance of the temple, the Divine Protection shall smile. Upon the shrine in the temple, the Supreme Illumination shall smile. Within the heart of the Deity, the Absolute Perfection shall smile.

At the United Nations, what I feel is an inner voyage. In its inner voyage the United Nations has to brave many temptations and setbacks. As we all know, defeats and failures are mere stepping-stones in our onward march to perfection. At the end of its voyage, there is every possibility that the United Nations will be the last word in human perfection. And then the United Nations can easily bloom in excellence and stand at the pinnacle of Divine Enlightenment.

WHAT IS THE UNITED NATIONS
REALLY DOING FOR HUMANITY?

*"My fellow inhabitants of this planet, let us take
our stand here in this assembly of nations. And
let us see if we, in our own time, can move the
world toward a just and lasting peace."*
                                        John F. Kennedy

What is the United Nations really doing for humanity? The United
Nations is humanity's colossal hope. The United Nations is Divinity's
lofty promise. Hope needs assurance from heaven's soul. Promise
needs receptivity from earth's heart.

Let us take the United Nations as a human being. Naturally, this
human being has a body, a vital, a mind, a heart and a soul. The
body of the United Nations is trying to serve humanity. The vital of
the United Nations is striving to energise humanity. The mind of
the United Nations is longing to inspire humanity. The heart of the
United Nations is crying to love humanity. Finally, the soul of the
United Nations is flying to embrace humanity.

The United Nations as a whole wants to offer peace. Peace and
the United Nations are inseparable. Now what is peace? Peace does
not mean the absence of war. Outwardly two countries may not
wage war, but if they inwardly treasure aggressive thoughts, hostile
thoughts, that is as good as war. Peace means the presence of harmony, love, satisfaction and oneness. Peace means a flood of love
in the world family. Peace means the unity of the universal heart
and the oneness of the universal soul.

To me, the United Nations is great. Why? Because it has high
principles. To me, the United Nations is good. Why? Because it
leaves no stone unturned to transform these principles into living
realities. To me, the United Nations is divine. Why? Because it is
the fond child of the Supreme dedicated to promoting world peace.

61

The world may notice a yawning gulf between the principles of the United Nations and the realities of the world. But the world must remember that in the transformation of principles into realities, time is a great factor. The world is old, and it has old ideas, old idiosyncrasies, old propensities. The United Nations is young, very young. Nevertheless, if we go deep within we can easily observe how many things have been accomplished in the brief years of the United Nations' existence. For the first thirteen years of our human life, we consciously or unconsciously wallowed in the pleasures of ignorance without even trying to live a better life, a higher life, a more fulfilling life. In order to live a higher life, an illumining life, a life that perfects and fulfills us, we need a great length of time.

We expect everything from the United Nations child, but we forget that the child has to grow. If we nourish the child, encourage the child and appreciate him for what he already has offered, only then will the progress of the child be satisfactory. If we place a very heavy load on the child's shoulders while he is still small and weak, whose fault is it if he cannot carry it? It is our fault. The child may think that he can carry the entire world on his shoulders, but the parents know that the child's wish will be fulfilled and manifested only in the course of time.

Unfortunately, the world is a bad parent. The world's pressures are attacking the United Nations, but the world's appreciation is rarely seen or heard. The way the United Nations has become a victim to the world's criticism is most deplorable. The world knows how to criticise, but the world does not know how to become one with the soul of the United Nations and see how hard its light is trying to come to the fore to establish a kingdom of Peace and Light on earth. The United Nations is trying to ameliorate the teeming afflictions that weigh so heavily on the world's shoulders. It is trying so hard to cancel the world's inequalities. The United Nations sings one song: the song that says it is love-power that will conquer the world. No other power can conquer the world. From this song we realise something more: when love-power conquers, the conquest is not for the expansion of influence, but for the illumination of existence.

The United Nations is the meeting place for the big brothers and the small brothers of the world. The big brothers are at times reluctant to share with the small brothers their capacities, their wisdom and their achievements. The little brothers at times want to grab the capacities, wisdom-light and achievements of the big brothers without working for them.

The big brother wants only one thing: satisfaction. The little brother also wants only one thing: satisfaction. Complete satisfaction dawns only when elder brother and younger brother smile simultaneously. If I smile because of my possession and you cannot smile because of your lack of achievement, I will have no real satisfaction. The smiles must be reciprocal, universal. The need of the younger brother and the abundant capacity of the older brother can be amalgamated. When they are united, both can together smile.

The younger brother wants nothing but acceptance; the older brother wants nothing but self-transcendence. Acceptance and self-transcendence are the prerequisites of action and perfection. Action means acceptance of the world, no matter how weak or insufficient it is, for its present and future transformation. Perfection means constant transcendence of today's achievement by means of self-giving. Self-giving is immediately followed by self-transcendence, and in self-transcendence only do we get the message of perfection.

People say the United Nations is imperfect. I ask what organisation on earth is perfect? They say the United Nations has not fulfilled human needs. I say we have not given full opportunity, not to speak of full authority, to the United Nations to do the needful. Imperfection is the fate of human organisations until divinity reigns supreme within them. There is no organisation which is totally perfect. But there are organisations which, knowing perfectly well they are imperfect, still pretend to be perfect. There are also human beings who know perfectly well that they are imperfect, but do not want to lift one finger to achieve perfection. Again, there are organisations and human beings that cry for perfection and work for perfection, for they know it is only perfection that can bring satisfaction. Without the least possible hesitation we can say that the heart of the United Nations is crying for perfection. In the inner world, the entire being of the United Nations is crying for perfection. But perfection is not a one-man game. It is a collective game that is played by all men. The capacities of all human beings have to be offered, as well as the capacities of all those who work for the United Nations.

After the First World War Woodrow Wilson and others had a lofty, sublime, supernal vision: a world united and at peace. The United Nations is trying to transform that vision into reality. Let us consider the vision as the height of Mount Everest, while the present reality is the foot of Mount Everest. We are now still at the foot of the mountain, but if we go deep within we will see that we have definitely climbed up a few metres, although we know how difficult it is to climb all the way to the top. Slowly and steadily the soul of the United Nations is offering its light to the body of the United Nations, which is the world, so that it can reach the height of the lofty vision seen when it was started. This vision cannot and will not always remain a vision, because inside the vision itself is reality. We can see the face of reality in four hundred years or in one hundred years or in fifty years or in ten years, depending on what the world sees and feels in the heart of the United Nations on the strength of its identification. And this identification can be achieved only if we live inside the soul.

Peace, freedom, progress, perfection—these are the four rungs of the cosmic ladder which the United Nations has perfectly housed in the unseen recesses of its heart. Peace we achieve when we do not expect anything from the world, but only give, give and give unconditionally what we have and what we are. Freedom we achieve only when we live in the soul's light. If we live in the light of the soul, if we can swim in the light of the soul's sea, immediately we grow into and achieve the true inner freedom. Progress we achieve by our self-expansion. How do we expand ourselves? We expand ourselves only by offering our inner concern, which comes directly from the very depths of our heart. Perfection we achieve only when we see the One in the many and the many in the One. When we see the One in the many, we have to feel that Silence-reality is holding the entire cosmos. When we see the many in the One, we have to feel that Sound-reality is nourishing the entire cosmos. Silence-reality is the soul and Sound-reality is the body of the United Nations. From the body of the United Nations we get the message of union. From the soul of the United Nations we get the message of perfection

If we want to know what the United Nations is really doing for humanity, each one of us has to ask himself or herself the same questions, for each of us represents humanity. Are we really seeing the bright side of the United Nations? Are we sincerely working for the fulfilment of the vision of the United Nations? Are we wholeheartedly trying to become one with the struggles of the United Nations? Are we deeply concerned about the United Nations and its role in the world community? If we can answer all these questions in the affirmative, then the soul of the United Nations is bound to reveal to us what it has already done for mankind, what it is doing for mankind and what it will be doing for mankind. What has it done? It has brought down the message of promise from the highest in Heaven. What is it doing? It is proclaiming this promise to the length and breadth of the world. What will it be doing? It will be manifesting this promise not only in and through the seekers after truth, light and perfection, but also in those who deliberately deny the potentialities, the capacities and the soul-realities of the United Nations.

The United Nations has a big heart. Irrespective of human attainment, irrespective of human assessment, it will offer its nectar-drink to each human being on earth. Its soul's offering will be felt first in the soul's world, the inner world. Then it will be seen in the outer world. Finally, it will be accepted wholeheartedly by the entire world.

THE UNITED NATIONS AS
AN INSTRUMENT OF HUMAN UNIFICATION

"Till the war-drum throbb'd no longer and the
battle-flags were furl'd,
In the Parliament of man, the Federation
of the world."

Tennyson

In this world we see that some people just talk, others talk and then act, others talk and act simultaneously, and still others only act and then let others talk for them. Finally, there is a type of person who just acts for the sake of action divine. This is the supreme category. Without the least possible hesitation, I would like to say that the United Nations belongs to this category.

The world is blind; it needs God-Vision. And the United Nations has God-Vision in abundant measure. The world is weak; it needs soul-power. And the United Nations has soul-power in abundant measure. The world is suffering; it needs heart-consolation. And the United Nations has heart-consolation in abundant measure.

With utmost love and humility, the seeker in me tells the world to talk less and listen more. Listen to whom? Not to me, but to the United Nations. The United Nations has much to offer in every field, so the world needs its constant, conscious, unfailing and unceasing advice. If the world does not believe in the soul-peace of the United Nations, how will the world believe in the heart-dedication of the United Nations?

The Creator is at once the Silence-seed and the Sound-tree. Silence-life is embodied in the soul of the United Nations, and Sound-life is embodied in the body of the United Nations. If the world does not believe in the Silence-life of the United Nations, how will the world believe in the Sound-life of the United Nations?

The outer reality is not always the real reality. The outer reality sometimes, if not always, deceives us. The outer reality very often comes to us in the form of temptation, whereas the inner reality comes to us in the form of emancipation, liberation and salvation. If from the outer reality we go to the inner reality to challenge and fight against it, then we are acting like a fool. The inner reality will never surrender to the outer reality. But if we become one with the inner reality, which is our Silence-life, which is God's Vision, then we can bring it to the fore and transform the outer reality. The outer reality is the reality created by the human mind, the mind which right now is imperfection incarnate. Again, this very mind will one day be transformed, perfected, divinised and immortalised. By whom? By the Inner Pilot and by the divine forces of the inner world.

Critics are of the opinion that the United Nations sometimes is not brave enough or quick enough. Now it is very easy to criticise an organisation. But we have to know what precisely an organisation is. An organisation is composed of human beings, and human beings are far, far from perfection. It is the human in us that criticises, not the divine in us. The divine in us sees the perfection in ourselves and in others. Who is our brother? He is our brother who sees the divine in us and the perfection in us. A real seeker feels that he is growing from perfection, to greater perfection, to infinite Perfection; from light, to more light, to abundant, infinite and immortal Light. Similarly the achievement of the United Nations in the outer world is the achievement of a perfection that is always becoming more perfect; and a day will come when it will be totally perfect.

There are many ways to serve the United Nations: with the physical body, the physical mind, the inner heart and the soul's good will. I wish to say that all the services rendered by each individual are necessary, for through them we all offer our perfection to the soul of the United Nations. Each individual not only has the message of perfection, but actually is the message of perfection. And if we can offer this message of perfection to the soul of the United Nations, then the capacity of the United Nations multiplies itself into infinity.

Let us not ask the United Nations what it has done. Let us not even ask ourselves what we have done. But let us only ask ourselves whether we are of the United Nations and for the United Nations. If we say we are of the United Nations, then our source is peace, infinite Peace. And if we say we are for the United Nations, then our manifestation is delight, eternal Delight. Our source is Peace and our manifestation is Bliss on earth. So if we know what we are and what we stand for, then the United Nations becomes for us the answer to world suffering, world darkness and world ignorance.

The inner vision of the United Nations is the gift supreme. This vision the world can deny for ten, twenty, thirty, forty, one hundred years. But a day will dawn when the vision of the United Nations will save the world. And when the reality of the United Nations starts bearing fruit, then the breath of Immortality will be a living reality on earth.

IS A SPIRITUAL ROLE FOR THE
UNITED NATIONS PRACTICAL?

*"Some men are just as firmly convinced of what
they think as others are of what they know."*
Aristotle

The United Nations is playing a most important role in seeking to
establish world harmony, world peace, world oneness, world
divinity, world perfection and God-satisfaction.

The outer world says that the United Nations is not strong
enough, but the inner world has something else to say. The inner
world says that the real capacity of the United Nations is its willingness and its inner cry.

The United Nations is crying for world peace; and this very act of
crying is its real capacity. The way of oneness that cries to lead us to
the ultimate destination: this is the United Nations. The cry itself is
its capacity and this capacity is of supreme importance.

True, this capacity cannot or does not meet with satisfaction-
reality all at once. I have the capacity to run, let us say, but I am
not at the destination. I have just left the starting point; my goal is
still ahead. Capacity does not mean immediate success or immediate victory. Capacity is continuous movement that eventually
leads us to our destined goal. Right now the United Nations is a
cry, a movement, a forward march, a forward adventure.

A runner is running. Just because the runner has not reached the
goal, this does not mean that the runner will fail. There is an appointed hour and at that appointed hour, which is God's choice
hour, the inner dream—the real dream—of the United Nations will
be transformed into reality. That dream is God's necessity to bring
about world peace. This is the inner necessity of the soul of the

United Nations and also its God-ordained responsibility.

The world may notice a yawning gulf between the principles of the United Nations and the realities of the world. But the world must remember that in the transformation of principles into realities, time is a great factor. The world is old, and it has old ideas, old idiosyncracies, old propensities. The United Nations is young, very young.

If we say that the United Nations is the result of the twentieth century awakening, then we are mistaken. The United Nations is the outgrowth of the inner awakening of human beings from time immemorial.

We expect everything from the United Nations, but we forget that the child has to grow. If we nourish the child, encourage the child and appreciate him for what he already has offered, only then will the progress of the child be satisfactory.

A spiritual goal for the United Nations: is it practical? Without the least possible hesitation I venture to say that it is highly practical. It is not only practical, but also practicable. Something more: it is inevitable.

We have to know what the spiritual goal for the United Nations is. Its goal is ultimately to become the saviour of the world's imperfection, the liberator of the world's destruction and the fulfiller of the world's aspiration.

THE UNITED NATIONS:
A NUCLEUS OF WORLDWIDE SPIRITUALITY

"There is no peace in the world today
because there is no peace in the minds
of men."
Secretary-General U-Thant

It is not only possible, but inevitable, that the United Nations will one day be a nucleus of worldwide spirituality. The symbol, the truth, the light that the United Nations embodies is bound to cover the length and breadth of the world. The United Nations that we see—the body and form— may not last. But the reality that is behind the United Nations, the dreams that each dedicated individual member has—not in his mind, but in his soul—have to fulfil themselves. It may take fifty, two hundred, or four hundred years, but the dreams must eventually be fulfilled even if the outer form, the structure, does not remain the same. But the essential thing is the soul's full blossoming into perfection, the expansion of 'United Nations' into 'Oneness-World'.

Previously there was the League of Nations; now we see the United Nations. A few things are changed and modified for the better. The League of Nations was Woodrow Wilson's dream. It no longer exists. Instead, it has blossomed into another dream, a greater dream. The United Nations is also a dream. And this dream will also eventually take a better and more fulfilling form. At that time it will be Oneness-World.

A League of Nations is like a cluster of flowers. A United Nations arranges the flowers harmoniously. When we have a Oneness-World, at that time we will not see several individual flowers; we will see all as one whole.

This outer form may not last, but there will always be another way of approaching the reality. And that reality is bound to dawn. It will dawn and we will have Oneness-World. This is God's Dream, God's Vision of Perfection. The Kingdom of Heaven that we talk about, that we have heard about, is Oneness-World, nothing else. Oneness-World must dawn. And even Oneness-World is not the ultimate thing in God's Vision. In God's Vision, oneness need not and cannot be total perfection. In oneness there should be constant aspiration to transcend. There are twenty members of a family and they have become one. But if there is no aspiration to grow higher, to grow deeper, to grow better, then that is not perfection. Even when oneness is established, we can't say that that is the end of the game. No, inside oneness there should be a continuous aspiration to go beyond, beyond, beyond. God's Vision is always a Self-transcending Reality, so after oneness we still have the message of continuous transcendence, which is real perfection.

So, first there was the League of Nations. Now we see the United Nations. From the United Nations we shall see the Oneness-World, and inside the Oneness-World we shall see the song of self-transcendence, world-transcendence, universal transcendence. And inside that transcendence we shall see perfection, which is satisfaction.

THE UNITED NATIONS AS A FORCE FOR PEACE

*"I am not an Athenian, nor am I a Greek. I am
a citizen of the World."*

Socrates

There are a number of things that the United Nations can teach us
how to share, but the four principal things are: the message of trust,
the message of concern, the message of unity in diversity and, finally,
the message of universal peace.

Each nation is unique in its own way. Each nation has achieved
something special, at least for itself. When a nation is ready to feel
that other nations are an extension of its own being, when a nation
becomes aware that all nations belong to one family, one source,
and have one common goal, then that particular nation can easily
teach or share its lofty achievements. Each nation knows inwardly
that satisfaction and perfection lie only in self-giving, not in dis-
playing its grandiose achievements or in hoarding its capacities.

All nations are pilgrims, eternal pilgrims, walking along the same
road, the road of Eternity. On the way, some become tired and
want to take rest. They do not have the energy to walk any farther.
At that moment, if the nations that are ahead can feed and energise
those that have fallen back, then the lagging ones can easily keep
pace with the nations that are marching speedily.

If a strong nation feels that its progress will be slow if it helps a
weak one, I wish to say that this is not true. If one nation encour-
ages, inspires, feeds and energises the nations that are behind,
then the gratitude-flower of those particular nations will blossom
inside the strong nation's heart, and the fragrance of the gratitude-
flower is bound to accelerate the strong nation's progress toward its

73

destined goal. The fragrance of the flower will inspire it, and from this inspiration it will get abundant life, abundant light and an abundant sense of achievement and perfection.

The great mystic thinker Kahlil Gibran once said something most soulfully true: "The significance of man is not in his attainment but in what he longs to attain." The present-day world has achieved quite a few significant things. It has acquired money-power, technology-power, machine-power, but unfortunately it has not acquired soul-power. It has acquired the power to destroy humanity, but this has not brought it any satisfaction. It longs for world peace, world harmony and world unity. It has the inner cry to love the world, to feel the heart of the world and to become one, inseparably one, with the world at large.

The past has not given us what we really need. Granted, the past was significant, but it pales when we measure it against what we want to become. What we are now is a semi-animal, but what we want to become is a full, complete and total God.

Dream and reality are two different things. Right now reality is most deplorable, and man's dream is a far cry. The reality that the United Nations can offer to the world at large is not quite satisfactory. But for that we cannot blame the United Nations: for that we must blame each individual person. Unless each human being cooperates most soulfully with the will of the United Nations, reality will remain a painful accident in life and dream will remain a chimerical castle in the air. Unless and until we become inseparably one with the ideals of the United Nations, we can never be happy and fulfilled. The United Nations can teach us how to share. If we do not share with others what we have and what we are, we are bound to feel unsatisfied, no matter what we achieve and what we grow into.

Millions of people know about the United Nations and admire its capacities, its willingness, its eagerness, its good will. But how many people are ready to become one with the soul of the United Nations? Millions of people can meet together, but if there is no soul's bond, no soul's unity, then all nations will prove to be veritable beggars. In the matter of inner strength, inner power and real achievement, thousands of minds, thousands of bodies, thousands of vital beings or emotional feelings can join together, but if the soul's bond is not established, there will always be loneliness. The soul of the United Nations has to be accepted by all nations, and only then will a sense of completeness, perfection and satisfaction be attained.

Each individual being, each man and woman, should feel that he or she belongs to all nations. That does not mean that one neglects one's own nation to devote attention exclusively to other nations. But each human being who has the energy and willingness to be of service to other nations will also have the willingness to serve his or her own country in ample measure. While serving one's own country, one has to feel that it is becoming one with other nations. You have to feel that your own arms are becoming one with your eyes. Your arms are your power of work, and your eyes are your power of vision. Your vision carries you to the length and breadth of the world, whereas your arms remain where you are. With your vision you see the needs of your brothers and sisters of the world. Then with your arms you have to work to fulfill those needs. You can do this only when you feel that you have gone far beyond your little family and have accepted the world-family as your very own.

If each individual in each nation can consciously and devotedly feel that he does not belong to a little family called "I and mine" but to a larger family called "We and ours,", then the message of the United Nations, the message of love, of brotherhood, of peace, of soulful sharing, can easily be received, embraced and executed by the entire world.

THE DIVINE MISSION

*"A great nation lowers itself to the smaller
and thus wins the smaller nations..."*
Tao Teh Ching

At the United Nations there are many missions representing different countries. To me each mission is like a river flowing into the ocean, and the ocean is the United Nations. Each mission is a flowing river entering into the ocean with hope, with eagerness and with a willingness to become part and parcel of the ocean. At the United Nations the Divine Mission flows not only in the ocean but also through each of the rivers. The Divine Mission of Light exists not only in the infinite Vast, but also in the tiniest drop of consciousness. In the perfection and fulfilment of the Divine Mission in the Infinite, and in the perfection and fulfilment of the Divine Mission in the finite, the Supreme Satisfaction will dawn.

In each of the rivers the Supreme Satisfaction has to dawn, for it is the constant flow of the rivers entering into the ocean that makes the ocean a living reality. And when the ocean flows back into the rivers, it offers them its abundant inner wealth so they can fulfill themselves through it.

The Mission of God in each permanent mission to the United Nations is as important as it is in the United Nations itself. The United Nations is the entire body and each mission is like a limb. The body is perfect only when all the limbs are perfect. If one limb remains imperfect, the body remains imperfect.

When we are really great we care for the small, for the poor, for the invalid. The mission of the great is to become one with those who are less great than they, and to lift them up to a higher standard through self-giving. The mission of those who are not yet great is to feel that the great ones are only the more evolved extensions of their own aspiring consciousness

5

A LIFE
OF
INNER
PEACE

A LIFE OF INNER PEACE

"Nothing can bring you peace but yourself."
                                        Emerson

Two lives: a life of aspiration and a life of desire. I have been in the life of desire. In that life I did not have even an iota of peace and bliss. Therefore, I entered consciously and soulfully into a new life, the life of aspiration. In my desire life, my existence was tossing in a shoreless sea, and it found its reality in a goalless shore. In order to swim in the sea of Reality, in order to reach the Golden Shore of the Beyond, I entered into the life of aspiration.

Some people think that a spiritual person is impractical but that is a mistake. On the contrary, a spiritual person is really practical. An ordinary, unaspiring person thinks of God as being in Heaven, millions and billions and trillions of miles higher than his own existence. His God is not around him, not in front of him, but in an unknown or unknowable Heaven.

But a spiritual person has a different idea of God. He says, "If God exists, then He has to be inside my heart, all around me, right in front of me." So a seeker is practical. He does not accept the theory that God is in a distant and unattainable Heaven, that God is aloof and uninterested in his life. He says, "Only if my God is right here on earth, will I be able to fulfil my aspiration and my need."

Once he realises that God is right in front of him, he immediately feels that God is everywhere, both in Heaven and on earth. When he thinks of God in Heaven, he immediately feels that God is reality.

In the ordinary life, there are many needs. But in the spiritual life we

81

come to realise that there is only one need, and that is a love for God.

A spiritual person is not only practical, but also normal and natural. Everything in his life is orderly. He goes from one to two to three, and not the other way around. First things come first. And what is the first thing? It is God, because God is the Creator, God is the Source. Every day dawns with a new life, a new hope, a new sense of Immortality. Now, when the morning dawns, the seeker does first things first. First he prays to God, then he thinks of mankind, and finally he thinks of himself.

When he prays or meditates on God, the seeker uses the divine instrument, surrender. "Let Thy Will be done," he says. And when he thinks of mankind, he uses the instrument, love. He uses his love-power, his love-instrument to become inseparably one with humanity. Then, when he thinks of himself, he uses his discipline-power, his self-control. If he uses his power of self-control, then at every moment a new dream can be dreamt by the divine within him, the seeker within him. A higher call from above takes him to his reality, which is ever-transcending.

As an individual, I have to know that my physical body is not my only reality. I also have a soul, a heart, a mind and a vital. I have to care for my soul first, because this is the eldest member of my family. The soul is constantly dreaming in and through me, and the dream of the soul is the harbinger of my reality's perfection. So I have to think of the soul or meditate on the soul first.

Next I think of my heart. My heart needs love; it needs to offer love and it needs to receive love. First it gives love, then it receives love and finally it becomes love itself. After giving and receiving love, my heart will feel its inseparable oneness with everything and everyone.

Then I have to think of my mind. If I just think of my mind, that does not solve any problem at all. I have to meditate on the mind with the idea of expanding and illumining it. I think not of the mind that binds me or limits me or separates me; I think of the mind that will gladly listen to the heart and to the soul, the mind that can feel the universal oneness.

Then I have to think of my vital. When I think of my vital, I have to think of dynamic energy. If there is no dynamic energy I cannot produce or achieve anything. Life is a river that flows constantly and continuously. Vital energy is the current that carries us to the sea, the sea of illumination and perfection.

When we think of the physical, immediately we think of the mind, because we feel that the mind is the most developed member of our family. This is true before we have accepted the spiritual life. But after we have accepted the spiritual life we feel that the heart is an older brother and superior to the mind. And when we become really spiritual, we can boldly say that we do not need the mind at all; that what we need is the heart and soul to guide us through life. Granted, the mind may have everything that the heart has. If we want a diamond, we can find a diamond in the mind-room, and we can find the same diamond in the heart-room. But the moment we enter into the mind-room we see that that room is full of rubbish, junk and undivine things. The diamond is covered, and it will take us days, months and years to uncover it. But when we enter into the heart-room, we see that there is nothing else but the diamond. The moment we open the door, the diamond is right there before us.

A spiritual person is a man of wisdom. Just by seeing the diamond, he will not be fully satisfied; he will want to grow into the diamond itself. This spiritual diamond is perfect Perfection. The spiritual person enters into the heart-room, sees the diamond, touches the diamond, meditates on the diamond and grows into the diamond. When he grows into the diamond, that means he has become the perfect instrument of God. Then his real satisfaction dawns. A seeker's satisfaction dawns only when he becomes a perfect instrument of the Supreme. At that time, he becomes one with earth-consciousness and one with Heaven-consciousness.

SPIRITUALITY IN PRACTICE

"The world is charged with the grandeur of God...
There lives the dearest freshness deep down things."
Hopkins

In the outer life you cannot have peace unless and until you have first established peace in your inner life. Early in the morning, if you treasure a few divine thoughts before leaving your home, these thoughts will enter into the outer life as energizing, fulfilling realities . But they perform their task only according to their capacity. The peace you get from the inner world you offer to the world at large. But the outer world does not want it; the outer world does not care for it. The outer world says it needs peace, but when you give the world the peace-fruit, it just throws the fruit aside.

In the morning you pray to God for peace, and then you go to work. There your colleagues, who have not prayed or meditated, are quarrelling and fighting. They are in another world. Now you may say, "I prayed for peace. How is it that my colleagues today are still quarrelling over minor things?" I wish to tell you that if you had not prayed for peace, it could have been infinitely worse. Your prayer has definitely made the situation better than it might have been. Again, if your prayer had been more intense, more soulful, then I wish to say that the turmoil in your particular department could have been less. And if you had had a most powerful meditation early in the morning, I assure you the power of your own prayer and meditation in the inner world could have easily averted the wrong forces, the misunderstanding, among your colleagues.

It is in the inner world that everything starts. The inner world is where we sow the seed. If we sow the seed of peace and love, naturally it will produce a tree of peace and love when it germinates. But if we don't sow the seed, then how are we going to have the plant or the tree? It is impossible! Unfortunately we do not all pray for peace. We pray for joy or for our personal satisfaction. Of course, it is true that we need these things. Today we may need joy, tomorrow we may need love, the day after tomorrow we may need the fulfilment of a particular desire. But again, there is a desire, an aspiration which everybody has, and that is the desire for peace.

The peace we try to bring forward from the outer world is not peace; it is only temporary compromise. You see the political situation. For a few months or years, two parties may remain at peace. They feel that while keeping an outer compromise they will secretly strengthen their capacity. Then, when they get the opportunity or when the vital urge compels them, they fight. I wait for the opportunity when I can more powerfully, most powerfully attack you. But the inner peace is a different matter. The peace we bring to the fore from the inner world through our prayer and meditation is very strong, very powerful, and it lasts. So when we have that peace in our inner life, the outer life is bound to be transformed. It is only a matter of time.

DOES MEDITATION REALLY ACCOMPLISH ANYTHING?

"No peace which is not peace for all..."
Dag Hammarskjöld

First of all, let us try to know and understand what meditation actually means. What is meditation? Meditation is man's inner movement and outer progress. Meditation is man's inner soulful promise and outer fruitful manifestation.

A man of no aspiration will dauntlessly ask, "Does meditation really accomplish anything?" A man of sterling faith and aspiration will confidently ask, "Is there anything on earth, in God's Creation, that meditation cannot accomplish? Is there anything that cannot be achieved by meditation?"

God will immediately answer these two questions. To the man who has no aspiration, God will say, "My child, sleep. Sleep. You need rest." To the one who is all aspiration, God will say, "My child, fly. Fly. My highest Height of the Transcendental Beyond is eagerly expecting your arrival."

What is the first and foremost thing we expect from meditation? Peace. Peace and nothing else. Meditation is the embodiment of peace. The present-day world needs only one thing: peace.

Why do we meditate? We meditate just because our life needs inspiration, our life needs aspiration. Aspiration is, to some extent, a form of meditation. It is our meditation that promises to give us our realisation-tree. Today meditation plays the role of aspiration and tomorrow meditation will play the role of realisation. The Inner Pilot, the Pilot Supreme within us, inspires us to act; and it is He who has already kept the fruit of action safe in the life of our aspiration.

In our human life two things are of paramount importance: role and Goal. At every moment we have to know what our role is, and then we have to be conscious of our ultimate Goal. At our journey's start we have to be fully aware of our role. At the end of our journey's close we have to be fully conscious of our Goal. Now, there must needs be a connecting link between our role and our Goal. Meditation is this connecting link between our role in the Divine Play, the Divine Lila, and our ultimate Goal in God's ever-evolving Universe. Man's role is his conscious self-surrender to the Will of the Absolute Supreme. This is his only role. Man's Goal, the Goal of Goals, is in constant self-surrender to the absolute Will of the Supreme.

Life is conscious ascent and conscious descent. Now, when we say ascent, what do we actually mean? Life's aspiration is ascending towards the Highest. When we say descent, we mean the illumining descent of the soul's all-transforming and all-fulfilling meditation. Human life is an ascending prayer. Again, the divine soul in each human being is a descending meditation. Our ascending cry and the descending Grace are inseparable. Together they move, together they fulfill the Absolute, here on earth. As human beings are countless, even so are their endless prayers. Each human being can doubt the value of spiritual prayer during his short span of life, but no human being on earth can say that he never prayed. Be it for a fleeting second or for hours or for months or for years, each individual has to pray. This prayer has intrinsic value. Again, when it is a matter of the individual, one individual can far excel the rest of mankind; similarly, one individual prayer far excels all prayer.

Does meditation accomplish anything? Meditation does accomplish something; in fact, it accomplishes everything. God's Divinity meditated and created humanity, humanity in infinite shapes and forms. God's humanity meditates, and before long we shall see the result: the sun of perfect Perfection will shine on the face of aspiring humanity.

MEDITATION: SELF-TRANSCENDENCE

"God is truth and light his shadow."
                                                    Plato

Meditation is self-transcendence. Self-transcendence is the message of the Beyond. The message of the Beyond is God, the eternally evolving Soul, and God, the eternally fulfilling Goal.

The animal in man is proud of his self-aggrandisement. The human in man is delighted with his self-awareness. The divine in man is conscious of his self-realisation. The Supreme in man is fulfilled in his self-transcendence.

Man needs material wealth to enjoy a prosperous earthly life. Man needs meditation to live a peaceful heavenly life. Man needs revelation to live as a divine hero, to guide and serve and serve and guide as a divine hero. Heaven does not want a weakling. Earth does not need a weakling.

Life is not empty talk. Life is not the breath of illusion. Life is the action of aspiration. Aspiration is the action of man's Inner Pilot. Let us fight the battle of life within. Let us wake up to the reality of our world consciously and devotedly. Ours will be the victory without. Forget we must not, never. We are of God the Infinite and we are for God the Eternal.

Meditation means the evolution of the body and the soul. The body's ultimate evolution is transformation and perfection. The soul's ultimate evolution is the highest illumination and complete manifestation.

He who meditates, consciously dedicates his life to God. He who dedicates his life to mankind, soulfully meditates on the real God.

His are the eyes that see Heaven on earth. In him divinity and humanity are triumphantly blended.

Temptation and meditation. Temptation: this is precisely what an unaspiring man knows. Meditation: this is what an aspiring man constantly is. An unaspiring man must descend in the scale of life and feel the very breath of ignorance. An aspiring man eternally ascends in the scale of life and lives in the very Heart of God.

We have hundreds of secrets, but meditation has only one: competence is achievement. Competence and achievement are the smiles of God's unconditional Grace.

Sri Krishna meditated. He became God, the Love Divine. The Buddha meditated. He became God, the Light Divine. The Christ meditated. He became God, the Compassion Divine. Now God wants you to meditate. He wants you to become God, the Life Divine.

INNER PEACE WITHIN SOCIETY

*"Be ye therefore perfect even as your Father
which is in heaven is perfect."*
New Testament

Some people think you must withdraw from life in order to achieve peace but they are making a serious mistake. In withdrawal your satisfaction will never dawn. It is in activity that we progress and achieve. It is in action, in fulfilment, in creation, in manifestation, that we can be satisfied. But we have to know that if we expect something from our action, peace will never come in our lives. If we expect some particular result from our action we will be frustrated when the result does not meet with our expectations. We will feel that we have failed. When this happens, naturally there can be no peace.

We have to feel that action itself is a great blessing, but the result of action we have to take as an experience. According to our own limited understanding, we see it as either failure or success. But in God's Eye, failure and success are both just experiences which help to develop our consciousness. When acting we have to expect only the fulfilment of God's Will. Whatever happens we should see as the experience that God wanted to give us. Today He may give us the experience of failure. Tomorrow He may give us another experience which will satisfy us outwardly. But if we live a spiritual life, no matter what result comes to us from our action, we shall be satisfied.

Let us look at a river. The river flows constantly towards the sea. It carries all kinds of rubbish—dirt, stones, leaves, sand—that it picks up as it moves toward its goal, but it always continues flowing toward the sea. We should also think of our lives as a river running to the sea. This sea is the sea of fulfilment. If we are afraid to act because we don't want to get involved with the imperfections of the world, if we become still and inactive, then we will never reach the goal.

You may say that you do not know where the goal is right now. No harm. Just move. If you go in the wrong direction, soon you will realise it and go in another direction. Eventually you will reach your goal. But if you do not move at all, there is absolutely no hope that you will go in the right direction. If you cannot do disinterested work, selfless work, then work with a motive first. If ego and vanity come in while you are helping someone, let them come. A day will dawn when you will feel that the satisfaction that you are getting is not enough. You will realise it does not last more than a few seconds. Then you will try to work in a more divine way.

Activity is always far better than inertia. Even if you run around like a mad elephant at first, eventually you will start acting like a deer and run straight towards your goal. You may start your movement with the crude and destructive strength of an elephant, but you will complete it with the grace and speed of a deer.

Action is our peaceful realisation.
Action is our peaceful fulfilment.
Action is our peaceful manifestation.

We have to act. If we withdraw from life then we are consciously and deliberately telling God that we do not want to be players in His game. God will allow us to withdraw for a few days or a few months or a few years. But then God will compel us to participate again, so He can fulfill Himself in us and through us. The world has to be accepted and faced. If we don't accept it, the world will remain as it is and then we will feel miserable that we have done nothing for the world.

FEAR OF THE INNER LIFE

"The only thing we have to fear is fear itself."
Franklin D. Roosevelt

Strange is this world of ours. Stranger is our human understanding. Strangest is our fear of the inner life.

Before you came into the world, before you donned the human cloak, you told God, your sweet Lord, with all the sincerity at your command, that you would participate in His divine *lila* (Drama). He said to you, "My child, fufill Me and fulfill yourself at the same time on earth." You were divinely thrilled; your joy knew no bounds. You said, "Father, I shall. May my soulful promise be worthy of Your compassionate Command."

As ill-luck would have it, you have now totally forgotten your promise. Here on earth you want to fulfill not God, but yourself. Your unlit mind prompts you to betray God. And you do it. You feel that God's fulfillment must come only through your fulfillment. If it does not work out that way, you are not prepared to sacrifice one iota of your life-breath to fulfill God here on earth. Your divine promise sheds bitter tears of failure. Needless to say, to try to fulfill yourself before you have fulfilled God is to put the cart before the horse. It is the height of absurdity.

Perhaps by now you have come to learn what has made you fail in your most sincere promise to God. It is your fear. If I ask you how many enemies you have, you will jump up and say, "Quite a few." But I have to say you are mistaken. You have just one enemy and that is all, even though, to your wide surprise, it seems like a host in itself. That single enemy of yours is fear, your unconsciously cherished fear.

You are afraid of the inner life. You feel that the moment you launch into the inner life you are lost, completely lost, like a babe in the woods. You may also think that in accepting the inner life, you are building castles in the air. Finally, you may feel that to accept the inner life is to throw your most precious life into the roaring mouth of a lion who will completely devour you and your outer life.

You have countless sweet dreams. You want to transform them into reality. All your dreams want to enjoy the world. You want to offer your momentous might to the world at large; but you feel that if you embark on the inner life, you will be deprived of all these invaluable achievements. So now it is time for fear to make its appearance, and naturally you start shying away from the inner life. Fear starts torturing you. It tries to limit and bind you.

Unfortunately, your life yields to this deplorable mistake. But if once, only once, with the help of your all-energizing meditation, you could carry your long-cherished fear into the inner world, you would see that fear loses its very existence there. In the twinkling of an eye, it becomes one with the dynamic strength of your inner life.

If you want to truly possess the outer world, you have to possess the inner world first. Not the other way around. If you want to truly enjoy the outer world, you must enjoy the inner world first. Not vice versa. If your heart pines to serve humanity, you have to serve the inner divinity first. Infallible is this truth.

PEACE IS OUR BIRTHRIGHT

*"How beautiful upon the mountains are the feet
of him that bringeth good tidings, that
publisheth peace.*
Old Testament

Outer peace and inner peace: outer peace is man's compromise; inner peace is man's fulfilment. Outer peace is man's satisfaction without being satisfied at all. Inner peace is man's satisfaction in being totally and supremely fulfilled.

How can outer peace have the same capacity as inner peace? Outer peace can have the same capacity if and when man's creation and God's Creation become inseparably one.

What is man's creation? Man's creation is fear. Man's creation is doubt. Man's creation is confusion. What is God's Creation? God's Creation is Love. God's Creation is Compassion. God's Creation is Concern.

Fear is the feeblest ant in man. Doubt is the wildest elephant in man. Confusion is the devouring tiger in man. There is no yawning gulf between man's cherished fear and his forced fear. Doubt God, forgiveness is granted. Doubt yourself, your complete destruction is decreed. Yesterday's confusion was the beginning of your insincerity. Today's confusion is the beginning of your insecurity. Tomorrow's confusion will be the beginning of your futility.

God's Love for man is man's aspiration. God's Compassion for man is man's salvation. God's Concern for man is man's perfection.

Man's fulfilling and fulfilled search for what is real is peace. God the Love is man's eternal Guest in the inmost recesses of his heart. God the Peace is man's eternal Host in the inmost recesses of his heart. That is why we can unfalteringly and unmistakably claim

94

that the loving and fulfilling peace is our birthright.

How can we have peace, even an iota of peace, in our outer life, amid the hustle and bustle of life and our multifarious activities? Easy: we have to choose the inner voice. Easy: we have to control our binding thoughts. Easy: we have to purify our impure emotions.

The inner voice is our guide. The binding thoughts are the dark and unpredictable weather. The impure emotion is the inner storm. We have to listen to the inner voice always. It is our sure protection. We have to be cautious of the binding thoughts. These thoughts have tremendous vitality. We must never allow them to swell into mountains. We have to face them and then dominate them. These thoughts are absolutely non-essential, and we have no time to fret over non-essentials. We have to refrain from the luxury of the emotional storm. Impure emotion is immediate frustration, and frustration is the harbinger of total destruction within and without.

How can we choose the inner voice? To choose the inner voice, we have to meditate early in the morning. To control and dominate our undivine thoughts, we have to meditate at noon. To purify our unlit, impure emotions, we have to meditate in the evening.

What is meditation? Meditation is man's constant awareness and conscious acceptance of God. Meditation is God's unconditional offering to man.

Peace is the beginning of love. Peace is the completion of truth. Peace is the return to the Source.

ILLUMINATION

"May Brahman protect us, may he guide us,
may he give us strength and right understanding.
May peace and love be with us all.
                                        The Upanishads

In this world there is only one thing worth having and that is illumination. In order to have illumination, we must have sincerity and humility. Unfortunately, in this world sincerity is long dead and humility is yet to be born. Let us try to revive our sincerity and let us try, on the strength of our aspiration, to expedite the birth of our humility. Then only will we be able to realise God.

Illumination is not something very far away. It is very close, it is just inside us. At every moment we can consciously grow into illumination through our inner progress. Inner progress is made through constant sacrifice. Sacrifice of what? Sacrifice of wrong, evil thoughts and wrong understanding of Truth. Sacrifice and renunciation go together. What are we going to renounce? The physical body, family, friends, relatives, our country, the world? No! We have to renounce our own ignorance, our own false ideas of God and Truth. Also, we have to sacrifice to God the result of each action. The divine vision no longer remains a far cry when we offer the result of our actions to the Inner Pilot.

In our day-to-day life, we very often speak of bondage and freedom. But realisation says that there is no such thing as bondage and freedom. What actually exists is consciousness—consciousness on various levels, consciousness enjoying itself in its various manifestations. In the field of manifestation, consciousness has different grades. Why do we pray? We pray because our prayer leads us from a lower degree of illumination to a higher degree. We pray because our prayer brings us closer to something pure, beautiful, inspiring and fulfilling. The highest illumination is God-realisation. This illumination must take place not only in the soul, but also in the heart, mind, vital and body as well. God-realisation is a conscious, complete and perfect union with God.

We want to love the world; the world wants to love us. We want to fulfill the world; the world wants to fulfill us. But there is no connecting link between us and the world. We feel that our existence and the world's existence are two totally different things. We think that the world is something separate from us. But in this we are making a deplorable mistake. What is the proper connecting link between us and the world? God. If we approach God first and see God in the world, then no matter how many millions of mistakes we make, the world will not only indulge our mistakes but will soulfully love us as well. Similarly, when we see the defects, weaknesses and imperfections of the world, we will be able to forgive the world and then inspire, energise and illumine the world just because we feel God's existence there.

If we do not see God in all our activities, frustration will loom large in our day-to-day life. No matter how sincerely we try to please the world, no matter how sincerely the world tries to please us, frustration will be found between our understanding and the world's understanding. The source of frustration is ignorance. Ignorance is the mother of devastating frustration, damaging frustration and strangling frustration. If we go deeper into ignorance, we see it is all a play of inconscience. Frustration can be removed totally from our lives only when we enter into the Source of all existence. When we enter into the Source of our own existence and the world's existence, we are approaching the Reality. This Reality is our constant Delight, and Delight is the Breath of God.

This world is neither mine nor yours nor anyone's. Never! It belongs to God, and God alone. So we have to be really wise. We have to go to the Possessor first and not to the possession. The possession is helpless; it can do nothing on its own. It is the Possessor that can do what He wants to do with His possession. So first we have to become one with God and then we shall automatically become one with God's possessions. When we become one with God and with His possessions, we can certainly and unmistakably feel that the world is ours and we are the world's.

Ignorance and illumination are like day and night. We have to bring illumination into ignorance-night. If we try to illumine ignorance the other way around, then the transformation of ignorance will be difficult, slow and uncertain. To enter into the field of ignorance is a negative path. If we pursue the path of darkness and try to find light in darkness, we are taking the negative path. The best way, the positive way to find light is to follow the path of Light, abundant Light, infinite Light. If we follow the path of Light, then illumination will assuredly dawn in us.

Let us look up and bring down the Light from above. The moment we look up, God's Grace descends. The very nature of God's Grace is to descend upon each individual on earth. When we want to go up to God with ignorance, it is like climbing up a mountain with a heavy bundle on our shoulders. Naturally it is a difficult task. Instead of doing that, we can remain at the foot of the mountain and cry for God's Grace, which is ready and eager to come down to us from the highest. Needless to say, for God to come down into our ignorance is infinitely easier than for us to carry our ignorance up to God.

6

POEMS AND APHORISMS ON PEACE

POEMS AND APHORISMS ON PEACE

A selection of Sri Chinmoy's peace poems and aphorisms follow. They have been grouped into four sections: Peace defined; peace attained; peace lost; and peace realized.

PEACE DEFINED

Man's fulfilling and fulfilled search for the Real is Peace.

☐

Peace is the beginning of love. Peace is the completion of truth. Peace is the return to the source.

☐

Victory and defeat are interwoven.
Do not try to separate them,
But try to go beyond them
If your heart longs for abiding peace.

☐

To commune with God, man has his silent meditation.
To commune with man, God has His urgent Peace.

☐

Will is power.
Realisation is peace.

Faithfulness waters the seed of Peace.
Devotedness waters the seed of Delight.

□

Our questioning and doubting mind is always wanting in peace.
Our loving and dedicated heart is always flooded with the inner
peace.

If our mind has all the questions, then our heart has all the
answers. The answers are perfect precisely because they come
straight from the soul that sees the Truth and lives in the Truth.
And Truth, Truth alone, is the Goal of Goals.

□

Delight is the divine bridge between Peace and Power.

□

Our heart needs delight and our mind needs peace, just as God
needs us to manifest Himself and we need God to fulfill ourselves.

□

God has infinite children, but the name of His fondest child is Peace.

□

A life of aspiration is a life of peace.
A life of aspiration is a life of bliss.

□

Man's goal is Peace.
Peace feeds him, his life inner and outer.

Peace is the perfection of one's mind and the divinisation of one's thoughts.

□

Peace is based on love: love for humanity and love for God. Peace is also founded on non-attachment. No thirst for gain, no fear of loss: lo, peace is yours.

Peace is also based on renunciation: not the renunciation of worldly possessions, but of limitations and ignorance. And that peace is the true peace which is not affected by the roaring of the world, outer or inner.

□

God has peace of mind because He has thrown away expectation.

□

Two infinite extremes: War and Peace.
War the destroyer of blooming worlds.
Peace the devourer of roaring wars.

□

Peace is God's constant Grace.
War is man's immediate disgrace.

□

PEACE ATTAINED

Meditation gives us inner peace. When we have this kind of peace, it is a solid rock within us.

The earthly turmoils—fear, doubt, worries—if they come will all be shattered. For inside is solid peace.

☐

You are telling me
That your life is committed to the future.
How do you then expect
To collect the rich harvest
Of today's reality's silence-peace?

☐

Peace begins when we come to realise that the world does not need our guidance.

☐

How can I have God's Light? I can have God's Light when I grow into the purest humility of the poor and the mightiest magnanimity of the rich.

My humility is my divine brotherhood. My magnanimity is my divine fatherhood.

□

At a certain stage in human development, when most of the people are not aspiring to be perfect, mediation is of great importance. It is a temporary mental relief, a pause, a rest in the life of the vital. It is a clever compromise. Therefore we must pay attention, reverential attention, to mediation.

But to expect abiding peace and illumining fulfilment from mediation is simply absurd. We cannot expect lasting peace and we must not expect everlasting, illumining fulfilment from mediation. For that we need meditation.

□

Ask your mind to be clever.
What your mind needs is peace,
And this peace it can get
Only from one place:
The heart of oneness,
And nowhere else.

□

Somewhere God's Peace can be seen.
True, but where?
In the illumining vastness of the mind.
Somewhere the divine Peace can be found.
True, but where?
The mind's complete silence knows the exact place.

□

107

A genuine seeker after peace must needs be a seeker after love. Love has another name: sacrifice.

When sacrifice is pure, love is sure. When love is divine, in sacrifice there can be no "mine," no "thine."

Love is the secret of oneness. Sacrifice is the strength of oneness.

□

If you sincerely want peace in the outer world, then offer all your wisdom.

If you sincerely want peace in the inner world, then offer all your silence.

□

A seeker of Peace desires beauty within.

□

If the individual consciously puts himself into the spontaneous flow of the experiences the soul wants to give him, he will eventually grow into abiding peace, joy and fulfilment.

□

"I need peace. Please tell me if there is any special time for me to meditate on peace."

Early in the evening, between six and seven, is the best time to meditate for peace. Nature, as it offers its salutations to the setting sun, will inspire you, comfort you and help you in achieving peace.

□

We are victims to doubt, fear and negative forces which we feel are quite normal and natural. Peace of mind is a far cry. We do not see a peaceful situation around us.

But those who practise meditation go deep within and see that there is real Peace, Light and Bliss.

We say "peace of mind." But actually we do not have peace in the mind.

By staying in the mind, we can never, never have even a glimpse of peace. If we want to have peace, we have to go beyond the realm of the mind.

□

If you remain calm and quiet and allow the Divine thoughts of your Spiritual Guide to enter into you, you will become flooded with Peace.

□

How can we have peace, even an iota of peace, in our outer life amid the hustle and bustle of life and our multifarious activities? Easy: we have to choose the inner voice.
Easy: we have to control our binding thoughts.
Easy: we have to purify our impure emotions.

□

In the outer world, the blind human body needs constant mediation. The wild human vital needs striking mediation. The unclear human mind needs illumining mediation. The weak human heart needs lasting mediation.

In the inner world, the fleeting, unaspiring human body needs constant meditation. The running, struggling vital needs striking meditation. The searching and climbing human mind needs illumining meditation. The crying and aspiring human heart needs everlasting meditation.

In the outer world, in this world of turmoil, mediation is necessary. In the inner world, in the world of frustration and despair, meditation is necessary.

If we can bring the result of meditation to the fore, mediation will have a different life, a new life that will be flooded with everlasting Peace, Light and Bliss.

PEACE LOST

A child is an orphan when he loses his father and mother.
A man is an orphan when he loses his inner joy—his Divine Mother, and his inner peace—his Divine Father.

☐

If peace is misused, it becomes idleness and lethargy.

☐

Pray to God to give you peace of mind so that you can see the Truth in totality.
   If you do not have peace of mind, wherever you are—whether in the subway or in Times Square or in the country—there will be no God for you.

☐

God gave me Peace. But I have lost it.
I have lost it because I have welcomed the restless vital horse to carry me to the worlds beyond.

☐

PEACE REALIZED

In our conscious awareness, in our conscious seeing of God's Presence, in our conscious feeling of inseparable oneness with Him, we shall establish here on earth, here and nowhere else, the Kingdom of Light, Truth, Peace and Delight.

☐

When we consciously feel God as our own, then at every moment in our inner life, in our inner existence, we feel boundless Peace. Outwardly we may be talking, we may be excited, but inwardly all is a Sea of Peace, Light and Delight.

If we bring down this Sea of Peace, Light and Delight into our physical beings, into our physical consciousness, then this realisation will be manifested on earth.

☐

O Soul! What do you do with your Infinite Peace?
"I feed the teeming vasts of the Past, Present and Future with my Infinite Peace."

A peace-loving man is a quarter-God. A peace-achieved man is a half-God. And a peace-revealing and peace-spreading man is a full God.

A peace-loving man is the serving God. A peace-achieved man is the glowing God. A peace-revealing and peace-spreading man is the fulfilling God in earthbound time.

□

Man's real goal is Truth. Truth awakens him from his ignorance-sleep. Man's real goal is Peace. Peace feeds him, his life inner and outer. Man's real goal is Bliss. Bliss immortalises him, his life-breath.

□

Peace achieved, fulfilment enjoyed, immortality employed: God forever caught.

□

Introduction is God the Love.
Conclusion is God the Peace.

□

Light received, Peace achieved, Truth revealed, Delight manifested. Then nothing remains undone.

□

When Peace is multiplied, Truth is multiplied.
When Truth is multiplied, Love is multiplied.
When Love is multiplied, God is multiplied.

□

Peace is fulfilled Delight.
Where Peace is, the light of Delight has replaced the right of ignorance-night.

☐

Harmony is sweet. Sweeter is Peace. Sweetest is Bliss.
Harmony removes fear of dire conflicts. Peace awakens our heart's divine confidence. Bliss establishes the reign of our divinely fruitful life.

☐

It is only through inner Peace that we can have true outer Freedom.

☐

Aspiration can be raised to meet the Peace from above.
But Peace must be brought down to remove one's difficulties.

☐

The revealing peace in the aspirant and the fulfilling power in the aspirant will clearly and convincingly make him feel that patience is the light of truth.

☐

To be sure, Peace is not the sole monopoly of heaven.
Our earth is extremely fertile. Here on earth we can grow Peace in measureless measure.

☐

7

AN AFTERWORD

AN AFTERWORD

Sri Chinmoy has conducted meditations at the United Nations twice a week since 1970. In his own words, he has introduced meditation *into the realm of* mediation, *and the three Secretaries General spanning his time there—U Thant, Kurt Waldheim and the present incumbent Javier Perez De Cuellar—have all expressed their appreciation of his work.*

U Thant offered him his gratitude for 'instilling moral and spiritual values' at the U.N. Waldheim also thanked him for his prayers for peace, telling him 'I know what you are doing for us. I can feel it.' And De Cuellar recently paid tribute to him, saying 'You concentrate on the truths and ideals which unite all mankind: the longing for peace, the need for compassion, the search for tolerance and understanding among men and women of all nations.'

Clearly his ability to inspire these men at the heart of the U.N.'s mission is impressive. It is that one word inspire *which perhaps best sums up his role there. Indeed, his most lasting contribution may be the urge toward peace he inspires in people from all walks of life.*

He has written, "Peace is the harmonious control of life." And the implication is that peace is not merely something static, passive. Rather it is a dynamic power, a force for change. He has also said, "Peace is the beginning of love. Peace is the completion of truth."

The heart is speaking. And people are listening.

Imprimé au Canada
Printed in Canada